OUR
HISTORY
HAS
ALWAYS
BEEN
CONTRABAND

OUR HISTORY HAS ALWAYS BEEN CONTRABAND

IN DEFENSE OF BLACK STUDIES

Edited by
Colin Kaepernick,
Robin D. G. Kelley, and
Keeanga-Yamahtta Taylor

Co-published in 2023 by
Haymarket Books
P.O. Box 180165
Chicago, IL 60618
773-583-7884
www.haymarketbooks.org
info@haymarketbooks.org
and
Kaepernick Publishing
www.kaepernickpublishing.com

ISBN: 979-888-890-057-4

See pages 171–73 for permissions information.

Distributed to the trade in the US through Consortium Book Sales and Distribution
(www.cbsd.com) and internationally through Ingram Publisher Services International (www.ingramcontent.com).

This book was published with the generous support of Marguerite Casey Foundation,
Lannan Foundation, and Wallace Action Fund.

Special discounts are available for bulk purchases by organizations and institutions.
Please email info@haymarketbooks.org for more information.

Cover photograph: Young women raise their fists in the Black Power salute at a civil
rights rally, circa 1968. © Flip Schulke/CORBIS/Corbis via Getty Images. Cover
design by Rachel Cohen.

Printed in Canada by union labor.

Library of Congress Cataloging-in-Publication data is available.

10 9 8 7 6 5 4 3 2 1

Contents

PART THREE: HOW WE FIGHT BACK

Preface

COLIN KAEPERNICK

> Black History cannot help but be politically oriented, for it
> tends towards the total redefinition of an experience which
> was highly political. Black History must be political, for it
> deals with the most political phenomenon of all, the struggle
> between the master and the slave, between the colonized
> and the colonizer, between the oppressed and the oppressor.
> And it recognizes that all histories of peoples participate in
> politics and are shaped by political and ideological views.
> —**Vincent Harding, 1970**

"**L**et's begin by saying that we are living through a very dangerous time." Originally penned in 1963, James Baldwin's words are just as relevant today as when first inked sixty years ago. From ongoing assaults on our bodies in the form of police terrorism and, more largely, the prison-industrial complex, to the denigration of our collective brilliance and generational resistance in the form of banning classroom content and curricula that centers Black people and our histories, we are under attack—and we are living through a very dangerous time.

While malignant strikes on the full and unabridged humanity of Black people is nothing new, the recent well-coordinated white supremacist counterinsurgency in the area of public education deserves our attention.

Early in 2021—in the context of debates over precisely what content from a piloted high school advanced placement (AP) African American Studies course would appear in the curriculum's final version—Florida governor Ron DeSantis proclaimed that African American Studies "lacks educational value."

His comments should be read both as a reassertion of white supremacy *and* as a clear invitation to other governors, state legislatures, and boards of education to ban or significantly augment curricula that centers the histories of Black people and an analysis of the relationship between systemic racism and the violent origins of the United States.

At the time of this writing, Florida and at least seventeen other states have laws or policies that restrict the teaching of race or racism. Make no mistake about it—attempted and achieved bans on the teaching of Black Studies throughout the country are more than an attack on Black people—they're also an assault on *all* social justice movements as well as non-Black people of color and white coconspirators fighting for a better, freer, and more just society.

We cannot and will not let agents of white supremacy dictate our future, our stories, and our humanity. We cannot and will not let this moment pass without chopping at the roots that allow white supremacy to metastasize.

My fellow editors and I—as well as the countless others who have given their time, talents, and labor to this project—are honored to share with you *Our History Has Always Been Contraband: In Defense of Black Studies*. Alongside powerful work being led by organizations like the African American Policy Forum, Dream Defenders, and cohorts upon cohorts of student organizers from around the country, I hope this collection of historical and contemporary essays—some of which are original—can be used as a resource to deepen our collective understanding of Black history through the discipline of Black Studies—a dynamic field of study whose twentieth-century origins were birthed in resistance to the very foundations of Western thought and the US university system. As Robin D. G. Kelley has recently written, Black Studies has helped to chronicle and analyze how Black communities have "tried to remake and re-envision the world through art, through ideas, through social movements, through literature, through study in action."

Our History Has Always Been Contraband is precisely this—it's study *in action*. As you make your way through this book, you'll notice that it is divided into three parts: 1: "How We Got Here," 2: "The History They Don't Want You to Know," and 3: "How We Fight Back." Part 1 offers a clear historical framework for understanding the "history of the present," that is, how accumulated histories of both oppression and resistance have shaped our present political moment. Part 2 is replete with essential readings in both Black

Studies and, more generally, Black history. Essays in Part 3 offer reflections on and practical steps for ensuring that our histories and the histories of white supremacy in the United States are included in any curriculum worthy of true educational value.

As Saidiya Hartman has elegantly asked, "What are the stories one tells in dark times?" This, in part, is the question that *Our History Has Always Been Contraband* helps to answer. My hope is that what's contained within these pages will help us to draw connections between past and present struggles and to find inspiration in our histories of community resistance. Yes—Black history in a society that refuses to shed its white supremacy *is* contraband. Yet, self-preservation is nonnegotiable. We must defend our stories, our community, our humanity, and our future no matter the cost.

PART ONE

HOW
WE
GOT
HERE

On Racial Justice, Black History, Critical Race Theory, and Other Felonious Ideas

ROBIN D. G. KELLEY

> [W]e fell under the leadership of those who would compromise with truth in the past in order to make peace in the present and guide policy in the future.
>
> —**W. E. B. Du Bois,** *Black Reconstruction in America*

> It is strange . . . that the friends of truth and the promoters of freedom have not risen up against the present propaganda in the schools and crushed it. This crusade is much more important than the anti-lynching movement, because there would be no lynching if it did not start in the schoolroom.
>
> —**Carter G. Woodson,** *The Mis-Education of the Negro*

On January 20, 2023, Florida education commissioner Manny Diaz Jr. tweeted out a chart justifying the state's decision to ban schools from teaching a newly created advanced placement course in African American Studies.[1] The graphic singled out the curriculum's inclusion of Black queer studies, intersectionality, Black feminist literary thought, reparations, and the Movement for Black Lives as "egregious violations of the law." It also identified scholars whose work was included in an earlier iteration of the curriculum as radical propagandists bent on smuggling critical race theory (CRT),

Marxism, and deviant sexuality into high school classrooms. Despite the fact that the College Board had not yet released the final curriculum to the public, Diaz as well as Florida governor Ron DeSantis claimed it violated Senate Bill 148, better known as the "Stop Wrongs to Our Kids and Employees Act," or the Stop W.O.K.E. Act.[2] Sponsored by Diaz and passed in April 2022, the law prohibits teaching anything that might cause "guilt, anguish, or other forms of psychological distress" or "indoctrinate or persuade students to a particular viewpoint that is inconsistent . . . with state academic standards." In other words, introducing and teaching race, gender, sexuality, and anything remotely resembling "critical race theory" was strictly prohibited.

When the College Board released the final curriculum eleven days later, it had changed substantially. Most of the material the Florida Department of Education (FDOE) found offensive was removed or downgraded from mandatory to optional topics. The revised 234-page curriculum eliminated queer studies, critical race theory, mass incarceration, and a section titled "Black Struggle in the 21st Century"; made the Black Lives Matter movement and reparations optional research projects; expanded its coverage of ancient African history; and added units on "Black Conservatism" and "Afrofuturism." The names of every offending author were removed, most of whom we've included in this book. The College Board insisted it did not bow to political pressure, despite a trove of email exchanges with the FDOE discussing potentially prohibited content and a final letter thanking the board for removing topics FDOE had deemed "discriminatory and historically fictional."[3] The fact is, the College Board stood to lose millions of dollars if the state of Florida canceled its AP courses. Although a federal judge blocked portions of the Stop W.O.K.E. Act that restricted academic freedom in public colleges and universities, the law still applies to private businesses and K–12 education, which would include the College Board.[4]

Rather than accept a watered-down curriculum bereft of the theories, concepts, and interdisciplinary methods central to Black Studies, students, teachers, scholars, and social justice activists fought back, organizing a nationwide day of action on May 3, 2023, calling out the College Board and defending the integrity of Black Studies. Apparently, it worked. A week before the national protest, the College Board announced plans to revise the curriculum yet again, pledging to restore some of the excised concepts and material. As of this writing, however, no specific changes have been announced.[5]

We put together *Our History Has Always Been Contraband* in response to the latest war on Black Studies, provoked in part by efforts to introduce an advanced placement course in African American Studies into our nation's high schools. We felt an urgent need to respond not only to right-wing lies and the whitewashing of US history but also to an ill-informed mainstream discourse over the meaning, purpose, and scholarly value of Black Studies. Despite the claims of even well-meaning and sympathetic pundits, Black Studies courses are not designed to serve Black students alone but all students. The point is not to raise self-esteem or make students feel guilty, nor is Black Studies merely a diversity project. The essays and collected readings gathered here should make it indisputably clear that Black Studies is a legitimate intellectual endeavor—one that that does not sit at the margins of social inquiry but at the very center.

Our History Has Always Been Contraband is intended for students, educators, and policy makers, as well as general readers interested in the subject and seeking to understand the politics behind the current attack on critical education. The readings are by no means meant to be comprehensive or representative of what is truly a vast interdisciplinary field. We deliberately selected texts and authors who had been excluded from the AP African American Studies curriculum, as well as a few canonical texts in African American Studies appropriate for high school students. While Black Studies is an interdisciplinary and *global* project, the latest version of the curriculum places a heavy emphasis on history centered on the US and precolonial Africa.

We chose to stress the interdisciplinarity of Black Studies by selecting readings that cut across and between literature, political theory, law, psychology, sociology, gender and sexuality studies, queer and feminist theory, as well as history. Works by Barbara Christian, Stuart Hall, Kimberlé Crenshaw, Saidiya Hartman, Khalil Gibran Muhammad, and others, exemplify how multidisciplinary and interdisciplinary scholarship help us understand the systems that govern our lives and what is required to change them. We also decided to spotlight the writings of insurgent Black intellectuals, such as David Walker, Frederick Douglass, Anna Julia Cooper, Zora Neale Hurston, W. E. B. Du Bois, C. L. R. James, James Baldwin, Barbara Smith, Toni Cade Bambara, bell hooks, and Angela Y. Davis. To read their work is to think with them, through manifold crises and toward liberation, however defined (that is, abolition, feminism, racial justice, economic empowerment, self-determination, desegregation, de-colonization, reparations, queer liberation, cultural and artistic freedom, and the like).

Black Studies itself has a history, and it is often a story of internal conflict and principled debate. To introduce students to this contested history, we've en-listed writings by Carter G. Woodson, Robert Allen, June Jordan, and Manning Marable. That most of the book is US-centered is an obvious limitation but a de-liberate choice given space limitations and our decision to produce a text that corresponds with the developing AP African American Studies curriculum.

THE LONG WAR

The right's vehement opposition to Black Studies is predictable. Black Studies has been under attack since its formal inception on college campuses in the late 1960s. We can go back even further. Most state laws prohibiting enslaved Af-ricans from learning to read and write were introduced *after* 1829, in response to the publication of David Walker's *Appeal to the Colored Citizens of the World*, an unrelenting attack on slavery and US hypocrisy for maintaining it. Back then the *Appeal* was contraband: anyone caught with it faced imprisonment or execution. Today, it is a foundational text in Black Studies.[6] Historian Jar-vis R. Givens found that during the Jim Crow era, Black school teachers often "deployed fugitive tactics" and risked losing their jobs in order to teach Black history.[7] In Mississippi, organizers with the Student Nonviolent Coordinating Committee (SNCC) taught contraband history in "Freedom Schools," while the Council of Federated Organizations (COFO) established "Freedom Li-braries" throughout the state stocked with donated books—many on Black history by Black authors. Between 1964 and 1965, white terrorists burned down the Freedom Libraries in Vicksburg, Laurel, and Indianola.[8]

Who's afraid of Black Studies? White supremacists, fascists, the rul-ing class, the status quo, and yes, even some liberals. As well they should be. Now, I'm not suggesting that *everything* done in the name of Black Studies is insurgent and challenges the social order. Like any other field of study, sharp divisions and disagreements abound. But unlike mainstream academic dis-ciplines, Black Studies was born out of a struggle for freedom and a genuine quest to understand the world in order to change it.[9] The object of study has been Black life, the structures that produce premature death, the ideologies that render Black people less than human and their material consequences, and the roles colonialism and slavery played in the emergence of modernity, presenting political and moral philosophy with its most fundamental challenge. Black Studies grew out of, and interrogates, the long struggle to secure our future as a people and for humanity by remaking and reenvisioning the world through ideas, art, and social movements. Consequently, it emerged as both an intellectual and political project, without national boundaries and borders. The late political theorist Cedric J. Robinson described Black Studies as "a critique of Western Civilization."[10]

A chief target of this critique has been the interpretation of history. Battles over the teaching of history are never purely intellectual contests between ignorance and "enlightenment," or reducible to demands to insert marginalized people into the curriculum.[11] Contrary to the common liberal complaint that schools "ignore" the history of slavery, racism, or anything having to do with Black and Native people—or more precisely, the figments of the white imagination they called "Negroes" and "Savages"—have long occupied a place in school history curricula. Generations of students learned that white people settled the wilderness, took rightful ownership of the land from bloodthirsty Indians who didn't know what to do with it, and brought the gift of civilization and democracy to North America and the rest of the world. During most of the twentieth century, students were taught that "Negroes" were perfectly happy as slaves, until some conniving Republicans and carpetbaggers persuaded them otherwise. Leading history books by Ivy League professors repeated the myth, and D. W. Griffith made the world's first epic film by depicting how the "great and noble" Ku Klux Klan saved America from the evils of Reconstruction. Of course, Black scholars and their allies consistently contested these narratives, an especially poignant example being W. E. B. Du Bois's epic text, *Black Reconstruction in America*, which included a final chapter calling out the ideological war on truth masquerading as objective scholarship. In "The Propaganda of History" (an excerpt is included in this collection), Du Bois believes in Reason but comes to see its futility in the face of white supremacy and colonial rule. Critical analysis did not prevail because he was writing against "one of the most stupendous efforts the world ever saw to discredit human beings, an effort involving universities, history, science, social life and religion."

Du Bois wasn't out to make a name for himself in the field of nineteenth-century US history. He was trying to understand the roots of fascism, in Europe and in his native land. And he witnessed the battle over the interpretation of history play out in the streets, state houses, courts, and newspapers for decades—often with deadly consequences. The rise of the second Ku Klux Klan in 1915 was inspired in part by a national campaign to erase the history of Reconstruction. The chief catalyst was Griffith's aforementioned masterwork of racist propaganda, *Birth of a Nation*, released in 1915 (the same year the renowned Black historian Carter G. Woodson founded the Association for the Study of Negro Life and History). Based on Thomas Dixon's racist novel, *The Clansman*, Griffith recast the rebels as saviors in white hoods who redeemed the South from rapacious, ignorant Negroes and shifty carpetbaggers, obliterating all vestiges of the Black struggle to bring genuine democracy to the South and the nation. Respectable white supremacists such as the Ladies Memorial Associations and the United Daughters of the Confederacy (founded in 1895) waged their own soft power campaign of building monuments to the defenders of slavery in the region and around the nation's capital. Note that the movement to erect statues celebrating Confederate war heroes took off in the early twentieth century, not immediately after the end of Reconstruction. Why? Because it took over three decades of white terrorism, political assassination, lynching, disfranchisement, and federal complicity to destroy the last vestiges of a biracial labor movement for white supremacy and Jim Crow to reign supreme. In other words, public monuments projected the same propaganda Du Bois found in the history books.[12]

REINVENTING CRITICAL RACE THEORY

What the right demonizes as CRT bears no resemblance to actual critical race theory, a four-decades-old body of work that interrogates why antidiscrimination law not only fails to remedy structural racism but further entrenches racial inequality. Racism, they argue, isn't just about individual bias or prejudice, but a social and political construct embedded in our legal system.[13] Taking a page straight from the old anticommunist playbook, the right has reduced CRT to an incendiary dog whistle in order to generate fear. In a textbook case of obfuscation, an antiracist academic project is turned into a *racist* plot to teach white children to hate themselves, their country, and their "race." The chief architect of this strategy is Christopher Rufo, currently a senior fellow at the archconservative Manhattan Institute, who, in the wake of the mass protests sparked by the killing of George Floyd, declared that the spread of critical race theory was behind the unrest. By his own admission, Rufo sought the "perfect villain" to mobilize opposition to the *anti*racist insurgency and had no qualms about distorting CRT to do it. Ignoring the scholarship while naming the scholars (notably the late Derrick Bell and Kimberlé Crenshaw), he presumed that these three words "strung together . . . connotes hostile, academic, divisive, race-obsessed, poisonous, elitist, anti-American." As he explained to his Twitter followers in 2021, the plan was to rebrand CRT and "eventually turn it toxic, as we put all of the various cultural insanities under that brand category. The goal is to have the public read something crazy in the newspaper and immediately think 'critical race theory.' We have decodified the term and will recodify it to annex the entire range of cultural constructions that are unpopular with Americans."[14]

Rufo's ploy soon became White House policy. In fact, Rufo helped draft Trump's (now-rescinded) Executive Order 13950, issued on September 22, 2020, which warned of a left-wing ideology on the horizon threatening "to infect core institutions of our country" by promoting "race or sex stereotyping or scapegoating."[15] The document pitted this invented ideology against the principles of "color blindness" derived from a distorted reading of Dr. Martin Luther King Jr. to justify eliminating workplace diversity and inclusion training in federal agencies. Rufo's popularization of a spurious definition of CRT, backed by the White House, helped spawn a wave of anti-CRT legislation. According to a recent study released by UCLA's Critical Race Studies Program, from the start of 2021 to the end of 2022, federal, state, and local legislative and governing bodies introduced 563 anti-CRT measures, more than half of which have been enacted or adopted. At least 94 percent of the successful measures target K–12 education, affecting nearly half of all public school children in the country.[16]

To be clear, these measures target not just CRT but liberal multiculturalism and, more pointedly, Black Studies, Ethnic Studies, Gender Studies, and any modern academic discipline that critically studies race and gender. (From here on I will refer to this scholarship collectively as "critical race and gender studies," make specific references to Black Studies or CRT when appropriate, and use "we" occasionally when explaining what scholars in these fields do.) Most of these bills share identical language because they derive from model legislation drafted by right-wing think tanks, including the America First Policy Institute, the Center for American Freedom, the Heritage Foundation, the American Enterprise Institute, Citizens for Renewing America, Alliance for Free Citizens, and the American Legislative Exchange, and the Ethics and Public Policy Center. It is ironic that bills allegedly intended to protect education from politics and defend academic freedom are backed by well-funded partisan think tanks. In fact, Stanley Kurtz, a leading critic of the African American AP course who masquerades as an investigative journalist for the *National Review*, ironically named the model anti-CRT legislation he drafted for the Ethics and Public Policy Center "the Partisanship Out of Civics Act."[17]

Much of the text was lifted from the section of Executive Order 13950 prohibiting the teaching of "divisive concepts." These concepts include the idea that one race or sex is "inherently superior" to others; that the US "is fundamentally racist or sexist"; that a person "by virtue of his or her race or sex, is inherently racist, sexist, or oppressive"; that "an individual, by virtue of his or her race or sex, bears responsibility for actions committed in the past by other members of the same race or sex"; that "meritocracy or traits such as a hard work ethic are racist or sexist, or were created by a particular race to oppress another race"; and that no student "should feel discomfort, guilt, anguish, or any other form of psychological distress on account of his or her race or sex."[18] The assumption here is that confronting the history of American racism would provoke feelings of guilt and shame in *white* kids (and their parents). Meanwhile, the psychological distress Black, Brown, and Indigenous students frequently endure as a result of a whitewashed curriculum, tracking, suspensions and expulsions on the slightest pretext, even abuses by law enforcement inside their own classrooms, is never considered.

Such allegations against critical race and gender studies strain credulity. No serious scholar believes that someone is "inherently racist, sexist, or oppressive, whether consciously or unconsciously, solely by virtue of his or her race or sex." Instead, we teach the opposite: that race is neither fixed nor biological but socially constructed. Modern categories of racial classification were European creations of the Enlightenment era that relied on a false science to claim that discrete "racial" groups share inherent traits or characteristics. We reject such claims as "essentialist" and recognize that behaviors and ideas attributed to race, gender, class, and sexuality are not inherent but ideological, and therefore dynamic and subject to change. The belief that hierarchies of race and gender are based on "inherent" characteristics is the basis for the ideologies of white supremacy and patriarchy. Such ideologies have been used to justify conquest, dispossession, slavery, segregation, the exclusion of women and Black people from the franchise, wage differentials based on race and gender, welfare and housing policies, marriage and family law, even the denial of women's right to bodily autonomy. Whereas many conservatives backing anti-CRT legislation actually subscribe to the idea that certain differences are "inherent" (that is, fixed and immutable) especially regarding gender, CRT and Black Studies do not. To put it bluntly, the argument that people are "inherently racist, sexist, or oppressive" *because of their race* is a gross tautology. CRT, on the other hand, uses evidence-based research to show that policies that further racial, class, and gender inequality need not be intentional, and that anyone—irrespective of race—can be antiracist. Likewise, to accuse CRT of teaching that "meritocracy or traits such as a hard work ethic" *are racist* literally turns its interpretation of US history on its head. What Black Studies and critical race theory reveal is the extent to which wealth was accrued through the labor and land of *others*. The foundational wealth of the country, concentrated in the hands of a few, was built on stolen land (Indigenous dispossession), stolen labor (slavery), and the exploitation of immigrant, female, and child labor whose lower status and vulnerability suppressed their wages considerably.

Finally, critical scholarship on race and gender categorically rejects the claim that any individual "bears responsibility for actions committed in the past by other members of the same race or sex." The language is intended as an attack on the idea of reparations, which does not claim that all present-day white people are "responsible" for slavery. Rather, the argument for reparations acknowledges that enslavement, land theft, wage theft, housing discrimination, and the like resulted in extracting wealth from some while directly accruing generational wealth to others. The same system of slavery and Jim Crow—or more precisely, racial capitalism—actually *suppressed* wages for white workers, and the threat of interracial worker and farmer unity compelled the Southern oligarchs to pass antilabor laws and crush unions. The end result was the subjugation of *all* working-class Southerners, including whites.

The right-wing movement to remake education is not limited to K–12. Nearly one-fifth of the 563 anti-CRT measures introduced and 12 percent of those enacted target colleges and universities.[19] We're seeing it play out in Florida as Governor DeSantis launched a successful coup against the administration of New College, replaced the board of trustees with handpicked allies, and has begun to totally overhaul the curriculum and wipe out all vestiges of diversity, equity, and inclusion. The latest attack on Florida's state university system, House Bill 999, is a flagrant attack on academic freedom and faculty governance. Among other things, it eliminates any major or minor associated in any way with "Critical Race Theory, Critical Race Studies, Critical Ethnic Studies, Radical Feminist Theory, Radical Gender Theory, Queer Theory, Critical Social Justice, or Intersectionality." It also prohibits faculty or staff from advocating for diversity, equity, and inclusion; promoting or participating in political or social activism; or granting "preferential treatment or special benefits to individuals on the basis of race, color, national origin, sex, disability, or religion." Responsibility for hiring all full-time professors is placed entirely in the hands of university board of trustees, the majority of which are governor appointees. The board may delegate its authority to the president, but no one "outside of the executive management team of the president's office" can participate in hiring decisions. In addition, it gives boards of trustees the power to review the tenure status of any faculty member on demand, which means even tenured professors are subject to arbitrary dismissal.[20]

Buried in this twenty-four-page bill and shrouded by the state's "anti-woke" rhetoric is another agenda. The governor and his Republican colleagues have advanced their plan to transform the state college system into an engine of market fundamentalism beholden to business interests. One of its objectives is "to promote the state's economic development" through new research, technology, patents, grants, and contracts that "generate state businesses of global importance," and to create "a resource rich academic environment that attracts high-technology business and venture capital to the state." In 2020, the governor and the state legislature established and lavishly funded the Adam Smith Center for Economic Freedom at Florida International University, tasked with promoting "a better understanding of the free enterprise system and its impact on individual freedom and human prosperity around the world, with a special emphasis on the United States and Latin America and the Caribbean." HB 999 further elevated the Adam Smith Center by giving it all of the powers of an academic department, including the ability to hire tenure-track faculty and grant degrees.[21]

THE REAL THREAT IS ANTIRACISM

A few days before issuing Executive Order 13950, Trump announced the formation of the federally funded 1776 Commission to promote "patriotic history" and
portray the US in a more positive light. Commission advisors blamed colleges
and universities for distorting history and promoting "destructive scholarship"
that sows "division, distrust, and hatred among citizens. . . . [I]t is the intellectual
force behind so much of the violence in our cities, suppression of free speech in
our universities, and defamation of our treasured national statues and symbols."[22]

The 1776 Commission found its "perfect villains" in the movement to
remove Confederate statues and other monuments to figures responsible for
slavery, colonialism, and racist violence: the late Howard Zinn's *A People's
History of the United States*, and Nikole Hannah-Jones's 1619 Project published the previous year by the *New York Times*. Conservatives and some liberal historians considered the 1619 Project an affront because it challenged
the founding myth that America was born out of a war for liberty against British tyranny. By reframing the nation's origin story to 1619, Hannah-Jones and
her fellow contributors contend that the US was built on a colonial economy based on racial slavery, plantation production, transatlantic commodity
trade, and the buying, selling, mortgaging, and insuring of human beings.
Rather than portray the so-called "founding fathers" as the downtrodden
fighting for liberty from colonial overlords, the 1619 Project exposes them as
the architects of settler colonialism. Consequently, the essays give the general
public a radically different perspective on what 1776 was about—a struggle
between factions of the same class over who would benefit from the spoils of
slavery, slave-produced commerce, and Indigenous dispossession.[23] The right
was having none of it. Several Republican-dominated state legislatures voted
to cut funding to schools that use materials or concepts from the 1619 Project,
and in 2021, Florida went further by imposing a blanket ban on material from
the project in *any* educational curriculum.[24]

The short-lived 1776 Commission issued its first and only report less than
two weeks after the January 6, 2021, insurrection on the Capitol building. It
models what the right is calling "patriotic history" and serves as a blueprint
for the current political attacks on Black Studies and all critical studies of race,
gender, and class. In sum, the forty-five-page document denigrated popular democracy, whitewashed the history of slavery, said nothing about Indigenous

peoples or dispossession, and claimed "progressivism" and "identity politics" were at odds with American values, not unlike communism and fascism. The report argued that the "founders" recognized "class conflict and tyranny of the majority" as the greatest threat to a republic and therefore curtailing democracy was necessary for the survival of the nation. On the issue of slavery, the report never discussed the institution, its character, its role in generating wealth, or its impact on democracy (for example, how the three-fifths compromise bolstered slaveholders' power in the Republic). Instead, it promotes the falsehood that the movement to abolish slavery began in the United States, and the founding fathers were its catalysts. The Declaration of Independence, the Constitution, and their crafters, the report argues, were fundamentally opposed to slavery, but the "practical" politics of holding the union together explain why the institution lasted so long.[25] Apparently, they were not opposed to the profits derived from the human trade or slave-produced commodities, certainly not the forty-one slave holders who signed the Declaration of Independence.

Perhaps their most egregious fabrication was turning Dr. Martin Luther King Jr., into a colorblind libertarian. The report managed to recast the civil rights movement as a proponent of individual liberty, equal opportunity, and colorblindness that, with the death of King, lost its way when it embraced "group rights," "preferential treatment" for minorities, and "identity politics."[26] This is the same Dr. King whose book *Why We Can't Wait* supported "compensatory or preferential treatment for the Negro" because, in his words, "it is obvious that if a man enters the starting line of a race three hundred years after another man, the first would have to perform some incredible feat in order to catch up."[27] The same Dr. King who called on the federal government to divest from the war in Vietnam, invest in the war on poverty, recognize racism as a source of inequality, and acknowledge "the debt that they owe a people who were kept in slavery two hundred and forty-four years."[28]

The stunning distortion of Dr. King's ideas should surprise no one, not even King. He knew something about the politics of history. On the occasion of W. E. B. Du Bois's hundredth birthday in 1968, King delivered a speech at Carnegie Hall on the significance of *Black Reconstruction* in challenging the "conscious and deliberate manipulation of history." Du Bois, King observed, proved that far from being "the tragic era" of misrule and corruption, Reconstruction "was the only period in which democracy existed in the South. This stunning fact was the reason the history books had to lie because to tell the truth would have acknowledged the Negroes' capacity to govern and fitness to build a finer nation in a creative relationship with poor whites."[29] A careful reader of Du Bois, King distilled in a few sentences why "the history books had to lie." Multiracial democracy, or what Du Bois called "abolition democracy," represented the greatest threat to the classes that ruled the South and the nation. It still does. DeSantis, Trump, Governors Greg Abbott and Kim Reynolds, the 1776 Commission, the Center for American Freedom, the American Enterprise Institute, the Ethics and Public Policy Center, and their copious allies all claim that their war on critical race and gender studies aims to present US history in a "positive light." If this were true, why not teach the history of movements that tried to make sure every person enjoyed freedom and safety, or that wanted to end slavery, Jim Crow, patriarchy, and sex discrimination? If "patriotic history" embraces the principles of freedom and democracy, why not introduce students to courageous people—like Benjamin Fletcher, Claudia Jones, C. L. R. James, Ella Baker, Fannie Lou Hamer, Johnnie Tillmon, George Jackson, Fran Beal, Barbara Smith, and others—who risked their lives to ensure freedom, democracy, and economic security for others? Why not create a curriculum centered on the abolitionist movement; Indigenous nations as early models for US constitutional democracy; how formerly enslaved people crushed the slaveholding republic, tried to democratize the South, and fought the terrorism of lynching, the Klan, and the Black Legion; how suffragists and organized labor expanded our democratic horizons and improved working conditions?

But in our current neofascist universe, this is what "woke" looks like. The right masks its distrust of multiracial democracy by calling it "progressivism" and its opposition to *antiracism* by labeling it "identity politics." According to this logic, *antiracism* has sullied America's noble tradition. Thus, *Ruby Bridges Goes to School, Martin Luther King, Jr., and the March on Washington* for young readers, Ibram X. Kendi's *How to Be an Antiracist*, and his children's book, *Antiracist Baby*, are targeted for bans and held up as subversive literature whereas there is no commensurate movement to ban books that *promote* racism.[30] For example, there are no calls to ban Thomas Jefferson's *Notes on the State of Virginia*, which asserts frequently that Black people are innately inferior to whites—physically, intellectually, and even in terms of imagination; Edmund Ruffin's defense of slavery, *The Political Economy of Slavery* (1853); or books and articles by Samuel Cartwright, Dr. Josiah Nott, George Fitzhugh, Louis Agassiz, Herbert Spencer,

Madison Grant, Lothrop Stoddard, or Daniel G. Brinton, the eminent Harvard anthropologist whose 1890 book *Races and Peoples* lamented, "That philanthropy is false, that religion is rotten, which would sanction a white woman enduring the embrace of a colored man." There are too many texts to name; and those listed above were not written by quacks but respected scholars.

The point of these attacks is to turn antiracists into the enemy or the perpetrator, and the people identified as "white" as the victim. Marginalized white working people, who *are* victims of stagnant wages, privatized health care, big pharma, and tax policies that redistribute wealth upward, are taught that they live in what was once the perfect country until the WOKE forces took over and gave their hard-earned income to Negroes and immigrants who are now trying to take their guns! In the anti-woke world of the extreme right, white nationalist vigilantes are the heroes, antiracist organizers the villains, democracy is the enemy of liberty, there are two genders, one civilization, one master race, and women and Black people know their place.

It would be a mistake to think of these attacks as a "culture war." This is a *political* battle. It is part and parcel of the right-wing war on democracy, reproductive rights, labor, the environment, land defenders and water protectors, the rights and safety of transgender and nonbinary people, asylum seekers, the undocumented, the unhoused, the poor, and the perpetual war on Black communities. The current fascist turn depends on controlling the historical narrative as a means of defining "American values" and identifying the alleged obstacles to making "America great again." As I write these words, the predominantly white Republican Mississippi state legislature is stripping the predominantly Black city of Jackson of political authority and revenue. Many of the same states adopting anti-CRT laws are also passing anti-trans bills and extreme abortion bans, and relaxing gun laws. The Tennessee state legislature expelled two young Black representatives, Justin Jones and Justin Pearson, for joining protesters demanding stricter gun laws after a mass shooting at a Nashville elementary school. And Texas governor Greg Abbott is planning to pardon Daniel Perry, who was convicted of killing antiracist activist Garrett Foster during a Black Lives Matter protest in 2020.

As we face a rising tide of fascism right now, remember how we got here: by protest, occupation, rebellion, and deep study. And as long as racism, sexism, homophobia, patriarchy, class oppression, and colonial domination persist, our critical analyses will always be considered criminal.

Black Studies Is Political, Radical, Indispensable, and Insurgent

KEEANGA-YAMAHTTA TAYLOR

For more than fifty years, the study of the culture, politics, and history of Black people has been present in one form or another in the country's colleges and universities. Its presence as an academic program and discipline came into being because of a national uprising of Black students in communities and college campuses. While the civil rights movement was driven by Black college students using their organizing muscle to end Jim Crow segregation at the lunch counters, movie theaters, swimming pools, and bus stations in the cities and towns they inhabited, by the end of the sixties, a new cohort of Black students returned to their campuses demanding classes that reflected their lives and histories, as well as Black faculty to teach them. Historian Martha Biondi has described the political moment as the "Black revolution on campus" when the unrest that upended cities across the country took hold first at institutions of higher learning, and later at high schools.

Of course, there had been Black history and teaching about the culture and lives of Black people in historically Black colleges and universities prior to the explosion of the Black liberation movement in the 1960s. But the Black liberation movement on campus was not just about introducing Black Studies into spaces where it had not previously existed. For Black students, it was just as much about politics and prolonging the struggle for Black liberation as it was about pedagogy and course credit. Young activists, fresh from the struggle in the streets against police brutality and substandard housing, brought the same militancy and verve to their battles on campus, but with the intent of leveraging the resources offered on campuses to build a stronger movement in the neighborhoods. For many,

Black Studies was not intended to build an "ebony tower" as an inversion of the "ivory tower." Instead, collegiate Black Studies was viewed as a political tool to educate Black people in their own history, politics, and culture to strengthen the political struggles among communities in proximity to these colleges and universities or the communities those Black and Brown students emerged from. In either case, Black Studies and the various ethnic studies programs that came in its wake, were, at their inception, political, radical, insurgent.

There was no contradiction between this political ethos and the educative value of Black Studies instruction. Indeed, instructors, prepared to distill the real, not whitewashed, history of Black Americans—as oppressed and exploited people, yes, but also as people who resisted and overthrew those conditions—instilled pride in their students, inspiring further learning. In the combative environment of the late sixties and early seventies, when many young people easily radicalized and believed themselves to be readying for "the revolution," Black Studies felt like an indispensable tool.

By the late 1970s and the early 1980s, that wave of revolutionary optimism gave way to the sobriety of a political backlash and a nadir of radical activism. Black Studies suffered political attacks but did not disappear. Instead, Black Studies, including Black Feminist Studies, became home to a wide variety of people who sought deeper understanding of the Black experience in the United States and beyond. The overall repression and decline of the movement changed the charged atmosphere through which Black Studies had developed. The insurgency of Black Studies may have waned, but it was still an important arena where US racism and imperialism could be critiqued and diaspora, culture, and resistance could be explored.

Black Studies today exists in Ivy League institutions as well as state universities, community colleges, and even some high schools. There are many more departments, rather than the less secure programs. Many of these departments are stewarded by highly credentialed Black academics. On many campuses, Black Studies has become an entrenched part of the academic status quo, no longer flaunting its radical lineage. Of course, there are still smaller programs and even smaller smatterings of course offerings in Black Studies that are typical at many more places, but the larger point is that it is rarely controversial to have courses that attempt to delve into the history, politics, or culture of Black people in the United States. That is, until recently.

When the *New York Times* published the 1619 Project to commemorate the four hundred years of Black people being present in the English colonies that eventually became the United States, it unleashed caustic, vitriolic, and frenzied attacks. It began with old, white historians complaining about the accuracy of Nikole Hannah-Jones's interpretation of the Revolutionary War and the role of slavery in the founding of the United States. By fall 2020, after months of uprisings and protests that brought a multiracial tide of millions into the streets against police brutality and racism, then president Donald Trump piled on the attack against the 1619 Project and what he described as "critical race theory." Trump bellowed in the months before the 2020 presidential election, "Critical race theory, the 1619 Project, and the crusade against American history is toxic propaganda, ideological poison that, if not removed, will dissolve the civic bonds that tie us together. It will destroy our country. That is why I recently banned trainings in this prejudiced ideology from the federal government and banned it in the strongest manner possible." He continued, "The only path to national unity is through our shared identity as Americans. . . . That is why it is so urgent that we finally restore patriotic education to our schools."[1]

Within the next few years, this attack on the teaching of or even discussion about racism in US history would swell into the efforts of lawmakers to legally ban or otherwise circumscribe curricula that examined either the history of racial oppression and exploitation or theoretical fields of study, including Black queer studies and Black feminism. Since January 2021, forty-four states have introduced bills or taken other steps that would restrict teaching critical race theory or limit how teachers can discuss racism and sexism, according to an *Education Week* analysis. Eighteen states have imposed these bans and restrictions. In winter 2023, the Republican governor of Florida, Ron DeSantis, banned an advanced placement course on African American Studies. In a post to Twitter explaining the rationale of the DeSantis administration, Manny Diaz Jr., director of education in Florida, said, "We do not accept woke indoctrination masquerading as education."[2] Elsewhere, DeSantis said that the AP African American Studies course was "inexplicably contrary to Florida law and significantly lacks educational value."[3] Following in DeSantis's steps, officials in Arkansas, North Dakota, Mississippi, and Virginia are also contemplating review of the AP curriculum for conflicts with their policies and laws restricting the teaching of the history of slavery and racism.[4]

The attack on Black Studies specifically, and the more general assault on the study of racism and slavery in US history, was not new, however, even though it was erupting in a new context. In 1974, Robert L. Allen, author of the essential Black Studies text *Black Awakening in Capitalist America*, wrote an essay titled "Politics of the Attack on Black Studies" (an excerpt of which is included in this collection). In the essay, Allen linked the attack against Black Studies on campus, exemplified by budget cuts and program closures, to the broader backlash against the Black movement. He wrote:

> Cutbacks were the means used to attack Black Studies, but they do not explain why this attack came. For this it is necessary to look to the larger political economy of which the educational system is a part. The attack on Black Studies coincided with the consolidation of reaction under the [Richard] Nixon regime. On the one hand, the domestic economy was in trouble, plagued by chronic stagnation, rampant inflation, and rising unemployment. On the other, the United States had been beaten in Vietnam and placed on the defensive internationally by the socialist countries, revolutionary struggles in the Third World, and contradictions with its capitalist allies.[5]

He went on describe the efforts of the Nixon administration, "as the mouthpiece of America's rulers," to launch "a campaign to shift the burden of economic instability onto the working population in general, while singling out blacks and other potential dissidents as scapegoats for intensified repression (code name: law and order)." Allen continued:

> Great efforts were made to convince any doubtful whites that (black) militants, (black) "welfare chiselers," (black) AFDC [Aid to Families with Dependent Children] mothers, (black) "criminals," (black) student radicals, etc., were the cause of the whites' present economic and political distress. This ideological assault served to cover the malicious attack (code name: benign neglect) being made against the black community as social welfare and education programs were slashed, public funding for housing undermined, and prices and unemployment allowed to skyrocket. Academic racists were trotted out and used to justify this attack on the "inherent inferiority" of the black race.[6]

Allen explained, however, that on campuses, the justification for the attack on Black Studies fell back on the "questionable academic validity"—as the critics put it—of Black Studies as an academic discipline. The critics argued that "Black Studies [is] political, not academic"; Black Studies "[is] intellectually bankrupt and [is] merely an attempt to boost the collective black psyche by glorifying black history"; and that "Black Studies is reverse racism."[7]

Almost fifty years later, these attacks are remarkably similar to the criticisms that we see—right down to the charge that teaching about Black history is intended to make white students, and white people more generally, feel guilty. There is also a similar context to the attacks on Black Studies. When Trump put the 1619 Project and critical race theory in his crosshairs, he desperately needed to pull the spotlight away from his role in whipping up a racist atmosphere—one that the 2020 protests forcefully responded to. Trump also needed to create some traction for his presidential reelection campaign, which was under threat of being engulfed by the growing momentum of the antiracist protests. However, that these attacks have now widened to target almost any invocation of racism in US history and gained a significant foothold show that this was more than a sideshow concocted by Trump.

As the streets swelled with protesters in 2020, the political idea of "systemic racism" once again took hold. The brutal murders of George Floyd and Breonna Taylor, combined with the well-reported ways the historic COVID-19 pandemic disproportionately impacted Black people (and the federal government's inept response), gave renewed validity to the notion of racism as systemic, structural, and ubiquitous in US society. This fresh reckoning opened the space for old remedies, including discussions about reparations. At the same time, the emergency COVID welfare state opened new possibilities for government to repair old inequities and address ongoing racism in our society. If systemic racism was real, then, perhaps, Black people were right in their claims to reparations. Maybe they were also right in the demands for more public programs to address these systemic, historic ills. These admissions would be costly and would come into conflict with both political parties' approach to governing, which for the last fifty years has been to denounce public spending for social welfare as wasteful while castigating those who receive it. Meanwhile, reparations in payment for the foundational role of enslaved people in building the United States has regularly been panned as outlandish. While there have been more sympathetic elected representatives within the Democratic Party, the ultimate failure of the Biden administration to make the COVID welfare state permanent, even while Democrats held a congressional majority, pointed to the steep political differences within the party over these questions. The denunciations from the right seek to delegitimize critical renderings of US history as either inaccurate or concerning themselves with events from so long ago that no one today can be held responsible.

Along these same lines, the right is attacking schools, education, and curricula because of concern about the radicalization of young white people in particular. Consider the concerns they express about what is happening in schools today. Former Trump secretary of education Betsy DeVos, commenting about the effects of the 1619 Project, said, "I think, there are a lot of young people—even my children's generation and younger—that probably have not been exposed to our history in a way that helps them really appreciate from whence we came and the need to protect what we have, to build on what we have, to acknowledge where we have to continue to improve. But not to forget what our foundations are."[8] In his 2020 Republican National Convention acceptance speech, Trump said, "Americans are exhausted, trying to keep up with the latest lists of approved words and phrases, and the ever more restrictive political decrees. Many things have a different name now, and the rules are constantly changing. . . . We want our sons and daughters to know the truth."[9] Trump continued, "America is the greatest and most exceptional nation in the history of the world. Our country wasn't built by cancel culture, speech codes, and crushing conformity. We are not a nation of timid spirits."[10] After Republicans did poorly in off-term elections in spring 2023, former right-wing Wisconsin governor Scott Walker wrote on Twitter, "Younger voters may be behind the stinging loss for conservatives in WI this week. In Nov, 18- to 29-year-old voters in WI went with the radical candidate by 40 points. Digital ads. Student coalitions. None of these will do it. We have to undo years of liberal indoctrination."[11]

This is why reactionaries have not just attacked Black history but look to replace it with their own version of history. As part of his tirade against the 1619 Project, Trump issued an executive order creating an eighteen-member commission "to better enable a rising generation to understand the history and principles of the founding of the United States in 1776."[12] At the heart of this effort is the reinterpretation of slavery and race in American life. Trump's executive order read: "The recent attacks on our founding have highlighted America's history related to race. These one-sided and divisive accounts too often ignore or fail to properly honor and recollect the great legacy of the American national experience—our country's valiant and successful effort to shake off the curse of slavery and to use the lessons of that struggle to guide our work toward equal rights for all citizens in the present."[13]

The order clarifies why this revision is so critical to governing today: "Without our common faith in the equal right of every individual American to life, liberty, and the pursuit of happiness, authoritarian visions of government and society could become increasingly alluring alternatives to self-government based on the consent of the people."[14] This is practically an admission that if it is true that the United States has systematically violated the rights of Black and Brown people throughout the history of this country (and in fact, around the world), then the entire American enterprise has been rendered illegitimate, including its stingy methods of governing when it comes to the social welfare and well-being of its most marginalized and exploited populations.

To this end, the argument that Black Studies is politics masquerading as academic inquiry is a smoke screen. Indeed, the problem is not one of politics mixing with education—the issue is *which* politics will be mixed with education. Were the state-sanctioned 1776 Commission to write history lessons highlighting the eternal goodness of all things American, that would be lauded. As Allen wrote in his 1974 essay,

> The academic world likes its veneer of gentility, but this only conceals furious struggles in which academics and politics are usually mixed. In this regard, the critics are right when they note that politics is a fundamental problem for the development of Black Studies. But the question is not politics or no politics; rather it is which politics? Whom will Black Studies serve? Will it be truly democratic in its intellectual and political vision, or will it become "apolitical" and acquiesce to a narrow, elitist and bourgeois view of education? This question lies at the heart of the present attack on Black Studies.[15]

During the 2020 protests, millions of young people clogged the streets—even in places where there was a negligible presence of Black or Brown people. Young white people face an insecure future of planet-altering climate change, suffocating debt, and low-wage, unfulfilling labor. The life expectancy of working-class white people is reversing—they are dying younger. As a result, young white people have become more sympathetic to the politics of social-ism. Many are interested in Bernie Sanders's campaigns and support Black Lives Matter as they offer ways of understanding the persistence of racism and inequality in our lives. Conservatives have very little to offer these young peo-ple other than the false salves of white supremacy and grievance.

In contrast, Black Studies offers a vital set of explanations for the per-sistence of racism in US society, as well as a spirited tradition of protest, rebel-lion, and resistance. The innovative areas of study that have evolved from Black Studies—Black queer studies, Black femii. sm, and Black geographies, to name but a few—also offer vigorous and expansive ways of thinking and understand-ing the world we inhabit, and different ways of seeing and knowing that come into stark conflict with the normative epistemologies that legitimize the exist-ing social order. This, of course, presents an existential threat to the status quo. By elucidating the history and experience of Black people, Black Studies offers a powerful rejection of the scaffolding of mythologies and lies that the United States has been built around. Those organizing lies and mythologies have also been used to justify the US's imperialist jaunts around the world.

The continued subjugation of Black people, which compelled tens of millions to rise in opposition in 2020, punctures the illusion of the notion of "American exceptionalism." More importantly, Black Studies lays fertile ground for creating sympathy, not antipathy, toward the millions of Black people who have been locked into abhorrent conditions because of racism. The 2020 protests showed a way out of the dead end of grievance politics that blames Black people for the conditions of economic privation that per-vade working-class white communities while promoting self-absorption and rampant individualism. Black Studies honors a tradition of resistance and struggle, potentially creating models for new social movements necessary to unravel a social order that rests on the destruction of the working class, in all its orientations and ethnicities.

Our History Has Always Been Contraband: In Defense of Black Studies il-luminates the powerfully variegated political and intellectual foundations of Black Studies by making accessible a collection of elemental writings that explore the richness of Black history over the last two centuries. Though the

selections included in this anthology aren't intended to be thought of as defini-
tive or exhaustive, they represent a useful springboard for ongoing exploration,
debate, and study of a history without which any curriculum ought to be considered incomplete.

PART TWO

THE HISTORY THEY DON'T WANT YOU TO KNOW

Walker's Appeal to the
Colored Citizens of the World (1829)

David Walker

*In 1829, David Walker, the son of an enslaved person who was born
free in North Carolina, moved to Boston. That same year, he published
a pamphlet,* Walker's Appeal to the Colored Citizens of the World,
*which became widely read and infuriated Southern enslavers. The state of
Georgia offered a reward of $10,000 to anyone who would deliver Walker
alive, and $1,000 to anyone who would kill him. Here is an excerpt.*

I ask the candid and unprejudiced of the whole world, to search the pages of
historians diligently, and see if [anyone] ever treated a set of human beings, as
the white Christians of America do us, the blacks.... I also ask the attention of
the world of mankind to the declaration of these very American people, of the
United States.

A DECLARATION MADE JULY 4, 1776.

It says,

> ... We hold these truths to be self evident—that all men are created
> equal, that they are endowed by their Creator with certain unalien-
> able rights: that among these, are life, liberty, and the pursuit of hap-
> piness; that, to secure these rights, governments are instituted among
> men, deriving their just powers from the consent of the governed;

that when ever any form of government becomes destructive of these ends, it is the right of the people to alter or to abolish it. . . .

See your Declaration Americans!!! Do you understand your own language? Hear your language, proclaimed to the world, July 4th, 1776—

We hold these truths to be self evident—that ALL men are created EQUAL!!! that they *are endowed by their Creator with certain unalienable rights;* that among these are life, *liberty,* and the pursuit of happiness!!!!!!!

Compare your own language above, extracted from your Declaration of Independence, with your cruelties and murders inflicted by your cruel and unmerciful fathers and yourselves on our fathers and on us—men who have never given your fathers or you the least provocation.

Now, Americans! I ask you candidly, was your sufferings under Great Britain, one hundredth part as cruel and tyrannical as you have rendered ours under you? . . . Some of the whites are ignorant enough to tell us, that we ought to be submissive to them that they may keep their feet on our throats. And if we do not submit to be beaten to death by them, we are bad creatures and of course must be damned, etc.

If any man wishes to hear this doctrine openly preached to us by the American preachers, let him go into the Southern and Western sections of this country—I do not speak from hear say—what I have written, is what I have seen and heard myself. . . .

The Americans may be as vigilant as they please, but they cannot be vigilant enough for the Lord, neither can they hide themselves, where he will not find and bring them out.

"The Meaning of July Fourth for the Negro"

(July 5, 1852)

Frederick Douglass

Internationally known abolitionist orator and writer, Frederick Dou-glass (~1818–1895) was born enslaved on Maryland's Eastern Shore. He escaped from slavery around his twentieth birthday and became a fixture on antislavery lecture tours across the United States. Known for his commanding oratory style, he quickly became a powerful voice for the abolitionist movement. On July 5, 1852, Douglass gave his now famous "The Meaning of July Fourth for the Negro" speech in Rochester, New York. In it, he underscores the contradiction between the holiday's celebration of freedom and the reality of bondage for so many across the nation. Here is an excerpt.

. . . I say it with a sad sense of the disparity between us. I am not included within the pale of this glorious anniversary! Your high independence only reveals the immeasurable distance between us. The blessings in which you, this day, rejoice, are not enjoyed in common.—The rich inheritance of justice, liberty, prosperity and independence, bequeathed by your fathers, is shared by you, not by me. The sunlight that brought light and healing to you, has brought stripes and death to me. This Fourth July is *yours*, not *mine*. *You* may rejoice, *I* must mourn. To drag a man in fetters into the grand illuminated temple of liberty, and call upon him to join you in joyous anthems, were inhuman mockery and sacrilegious irony. Do you mean, citizens, to mock me, by asking me to speak to-day? If so, there is a parallel to your conduct. And let me warn you that it is dangerous to copy the example of a nation whose crimes, towering up to heaven, were thrown down by the breath of the Almighty, burying that nation in irrevocable ruin! I can to-day take up the plaintive lament of a peeled and woe-smitten people!

"By the rivers of Babylon, there we sat down. Yea! we wept when we remembered Zion. We hanged our harps upon the willows in the midst thereof. For there, they that carried us away captive, required of us a song; and they who wasted us required of us mirth, saying, Sing us one of the songs of Zion. How can we sing the Lord's song in a strange land? If I forget thee, O Jerusalem, let my right hand forget her cunning. If I do not remember thee, let my tongue cleave to the roof of my mouth."

Fellow-citizens, above your national, tumultuous joy, I hear the mournful wail of millions! whose chains, heavy and grievous yesterday, are, to-day, rendered more intolerable by the jubilee shouts that reach them. If I do forget, if I do not faithfully remember those bleeding children of sorrow this day, "may my right hand forget her cunning, and may my tongue cleave to the roof of my mouth!" To forget them, to pass lightly over their wrongs, and to chime in with the popular theme, would be treason most scandalous and shocking, and would make me a reproach before God and the world. My subject, then, fellow-citizens, is American slavery. I shall see this day and its popular characteristics from the slave's point of view. Standing there identified with the American bondman, making his wrongs mine, I do not hesitate to declare, with all my soul, that the character and conduct of this nation never looked blacker to me than on this 4th of July! Whether we turn to the declarations of the past, or to the professions of the present, the conduct of the nation seems equally hideous and revolting. America is false to the past, false to the present, and solemnly binds herself to be false to the future. Standing with God and the crushed and bleeding slave on this occasion, I will, in the name of humanity which is outraged, in the name of liberty which is fettered, in the name of the constitution and the Bible which are disregarded and trampled upon, dare to call in question and to denounce, with all the emphasis I can command, everything that serves to perpetuate slavery— the great sin and shame of America! "I will not equivocate; I will not excuse"; I will use the severest language I can command; and yet not one word shall escape me that any man, whose judgment is not blinded by prejudice, or who is not at heart a slaveholder, shall not confess to be right and just.

But I fancy I hear some one of my audience say, "It is just in this circumstance that you and your brother abolitionists fail to make a favorable impression on the public mind. Would you argue more, and denounce less; would you persuade more, and rebuke less; your cause would be much more likely to succeed." But, I submit, where all is plain there is nothing to be argued. What point in the anti-slavery creed would you have me argue? On what branch of the subject do the people of this country need light? Must I undertake to prove that the slave is a man? That point is conceded already. Nobody doubts it. The slave-holders themselves acknowledge it in the enactment of laws for their government. They acknowledge it when they punish disobedience on the part of the slave. There are seventy-two crimes in the State of Virginia which, if committed by a black man (no matter how ignorant he be), subject him to the punishment of death; while only two of the same crimes will subject a white man to the like punishment. What is this but the acknowledgment that the slave is a moral, intellectual, and responsible being? The manhood of the slave is conceded. It is admitted in the fact that Southern statute books are covered with enactments forbidding, under severe fines and penalties, the teaching of the slave to read or to write. When you can point to any such laws in reference to the beasts of the field, then I may consent to argue the manhood of the slave. When the dogs in your streets, when the fowls of the air, when the cattle on your hills, when the fish of the sea, and the reptiles that crawl, shall be unable to distinguish the slave from a brute, *then* will I argue with you that the slave is a man!

For the present, it is enough to affirm the equal manhood of the Negro race. Is it not astonishing that, while we are ploughing, planting, and reaping, using all kinds of mechanical tools, erecting houses, constructing bridges, building ships, working in metals of brass, iron, copper, silver and gold; that, while we are reading, writing and ciphering, acting as clerks, merchants and secretaries, having among us lawyers, doctors, ministers, poets, authors, editors, orators and teachers; that, while we are engaged in all manner of enterprises common to other men, digging gold in California, capturing the whale in the Pacific, feeding sheep and cattle on the hill-side, living, moving, acting, thinking, planning, living in families as husbands, wives and children, and, above all, confessing and worshipping the Christian's God, and looking hopefully for life and immortality beyond the grave, we are called upon to prove that we are men!

Would you have me argue that man is entitled to liberty? that he is the rightful owner of his own body? You have already declared it. Must I argue the wrongfulness of slavery? Is that a question for Republicans? Is it to be settled by the rules of logic and argumentation, as a matter beset with great difficulty, involving a doubtful application of the principle of justice, hard to be understood? How should I look to-day, in the presence of Americans, dividing, and subdividing a discourse, to show that men have a natural right to freedom? speaking of it relatively and positively, negatively and affirmatively. To do so, would be to make myself ridiculous, and to offer an insult to your understanding.—There is not a man beneath the canopy of heaven that does not know that slavery is wrong *for him.*

What, am I to argue that it is wrong to make men brutes, to rob them of their liberty, to work them without wages, to keep them ignorant of their relations to their fellow men, to beat them with sticks, to flay their flesh with the lash, to load their limbs with irons, to hunt them with dogs, to sell them at auction, to sunder their families, to knock out their teeth, to burn their flesh, to starve them into obedience and submission to their masters? Must I argue that a system thus marked with blood, and stained with pollution, is *wrong*? No! I will not. I have better employment for my time and strength than such arguments would imply.

What, then, remains to be argued? Is it that slavery is not divine; that God did not establish it; that our doctors of divinity are mistaken? There is blasphemy in the thought. That which is inhuman, cannot be divine! *Who* can reason on such a proposition? They that can, may; I cannot. The time for such argument is passed.

At a time like this, scorching irony, not convincing argument, is needed. O! had I the ability, and could reach the nation's ear, I would, to-day, pour out a fiery stream of biting ridicule, blasting reproach, withering sarcasm, and stern rebuke. For it is not light that is needed, but fire; it is not the gentle shower, but thunder. We need the storm, the whirlwind, and the earthquake. The feeling of the nation must be quickened; the conscience of the nation must be roused; the propriety of the nation must be startled; the hypocrisy of the nation must be exposed; and its crimes against God and man must be proclaimed and denounced.

What, to the American slave, is your 4th of July? I answer; a day that reveals to him, more than all other days in the year, the gross injustice and cruelty to which he is the constant victim. To him, your celebration is a sham; your boasted liberty, an unholy license; your national greatness, swelling vanity; your sounds of rejoicing are empty and heartless; your denunciation of tyrants, brass fronted impudence; your shouts of liberty and equality, hollow mockery; your prayers and hymns, your sermons and thanksgivings, with all your religious parade and solemnity, are, to Him, mere bombast, fraud, deception, impiety, and hypocrisy—a thin veil to cover up crimes which would disgrace a nation of savages. There is not a nation on the earth guilty of practices more shocking and bloody than are the people of the United States, at this very hour.

"The New Master and Mistress"

from *Incidents in the Life of a Slave Girl* (1861)

Harriet Jacobs

*Abolitionist writer and autobiographer Harriet Jacobs (1813–1897)
was born enslaved in North Carolina and escaped to freedom in 1842.
Jacobs self-published* Incidents in the Life of a Slave Girl *in 1861 in
which she recounts the brutal treatment she experienced at the hands
of her enslaver. Her autobiography is widely considered one of the
earliest and most comprehensive narratives written by an enslaved
woman. Here is an excerpt.*

When I had been in the family a few weeks, one of the plantation slaves was
brought to town, by order of his master. It was near night when he arrived, and
Dr. Flint ordered him to be taken to the work house, and tied up to the joist, so
that his feet would just escape the ground. In that situation he was to wait till the
doctor had taken his tea. I shall never forget that night. Never before, in my life,
had I heard hundreds of blows fall, in succession, on a human being. His pite-
ous groans, and his "O, pray don't, massa," rang in my ear for months afterwards.
There were many conjectures as to the cause of this terrible punishment. Some
said master accused him of stealing corn; others said the slave had quarrelled
with his wife, in presence of the overseer, and had accused his master of being
the father of her child. They were both black, and the child was very fair.

I went into the work house next morning, and saw the cowhide still wet
with blood, and the boards all covered with gore. The poor man lived, and con-

tinued to quarrel with his wife. A few months afterwards Dr. Flint handed them both over to a slave-trader. The guilty man put their value into his pocket, and had the satisfaction of knowing that they were out of sight and hearing. When the mother was delivered into the trader's hands, she said, "You *promised* to treat me well." To which he replied, "You have let your tongue run too far; damn you!" She had forgotten that it was a crime for a slave to tell who was the father of her child.

From others than the master persecution also comes in such cases. I once saw a young slave girl dying soon after the birth of a child nearly white. In her agony she cried out, "O Lord, come and take me!" Her mistress stood by, and mocked at her like an incarnate fiend. "You suffer, do you?" she exclaimed. "I am glad of it. You deserve it all, and more too."

The girl's mother said, "The baby is dead, thank God; and I hope my poor child will soon be in heaven, too."

"Heaven!" retorted the mistress. "There is no such place for the like of her and her bastard."

The poor mother turned away, sobbing. Her dying daughter called her, feebly, and as she bent over her, I heard her say, "Don't grieve so, mother; God knows all about it; and HE will have mercy upon me."

Her sufferings, afterwards, became so intense, that her mistress felt unable to stay; but when she left the room, the scornful smile was still on her lips. Seven children called her mother. The poor black woman had but the one child, whose eyes she saw closing in death, while she thanked God for taking her away from the greater bitterness of life.

"Our Raison D'être" from *A Voice from the South*

(1892)

Anna Julia Cooper

Born into bondage in North Carolina, Anna Julia Cooper (1858–1964) is known for being a teacher, writer, and traveling lecturer. She published her first book, A Voice from the South by a Black Woman of the South, *in 1892. In it, she calls for equal education for Black women across the South. She also helped found the Colored Women's League (1892) and served on the organizing committee of the first Pan-African Conference (1900). Here is the preface, "Our Raison D'être," from* A Voice from the South.

In the clash and clatter of our American Conflict, it has been said that the South remains Silent. Like the Sphinx she inspires vociferous disputation, but herself takes little part in the noisy controversy. One muffled strain in the Silent South, a jarring chord and a vague and uncomprehended cadenza has been and still is the Negro. And of that muffled chord, the one mute and voiceless note has been the sadly expectant Black Woman,

> An infant crying in the night,
> An infant crying for the light;
> And with *no language—but a cry.*

The colored man's inheritance and apportionment is still the sombre crux, the perplexing *cul de sac* of the nation,—the dumb skeleton in the closet pro-

voking ceaseless harangues, indeed, but little understood and seldom consult-
ed. Attorneys for the plaintiff and attorneys for the defendant, with bungling
gaucherie have analyzed and dissected, theorized and synthesized with sublime
ignorance or pathetic misapprehension of counsel from the black client. One
important witness has not yet been heard from. The summing up of the evidence deposed, and the charge to the jury have been made—but no word from
the Black Woman.

It is because I believe the American people to be conscientiously committed to a fair trial and ungarbled evidence, and because I feel it essential to a
perfect understanding and an equitable verdict that truth from *each* standpoint
be presented at the bar,—that this little Voice, has been added to the already
full chorus. The "other side" has not been represented by one who "lives there."
And not many can more sensibly realize and more accurately tell the weight
and the fret of the "long dull pain" than the open-eyed but hitherto voiceless
Black Woman of America.

The feverish agitation, the perfervid energy, the busy objectivity of the
more turbulent life of our men serves, it may be, at once to cloud or color their
vision somewhat, and as well to relieve the smart and deaden the pain for them.
Their voice is in consequence not always temperate and calm, and at the same
time radically corrective and sanatory. At any rate, as our Caucasian barristers
are not to blame if they cannot *quite* put themselves in the dark man's place, neither should the dark man be wholly expected fully and adequately to reproduce
the exact Voice of the Black Woman.

Delicately sensitive at every pore to social atmospheric conditions, her
calorimeter may well be studied in the interest of accuracy and fairness in di-
agnosing what is often conceded to be a "puzzling" case. If these broken utter-
ances can in any way help to a clearer vision and a truer pulse-beat in studying
our Nation's Problem, this Voice by a Black Woman of the South will not have
been raised in vain.

"Introduction" from *Barracoon: The Story of the Last "Black Cargo"* (1931)

Zora Neale Hurston

Acclaimed novelist, essayist, anthropologist, playwright, and filmmaker Zora Neale Hurston (1891–1960) was a central figure of the Harlem Renaissance. Though completed in 1931, Hurston's Barracoon *wasn't published until 2018. Based on personal interviews, she explores the life of Cudjo Lewis, one of the last adult survivors of the Atlantic slave trade. Here is an excerpt.*

The African slave trade is the most dramatic chapter in the story of human existence. Therefore a great literature has grown up about it. Innumerable books and papers have been written. These are supplemented by the vast lore that has been blown by the breath of inarticulate ones across the seas and lands of the world.

Those who justified slaving on various grounds have had their say. Among these are several slave runners who have boasted of their exploits in the contraband flesh. Those who stood aloof in loathing have cried out against it in lengthy volumes.

All the talk, printed and spoken, has had to do with ships and rations; with sail and weather; with ruses and piracy and balls between wind and water; with native kings and bargains sharp and sinful on both sides; with tribal wars and slave factories and red massacres and all the machinations necessary to stock a barracoon with African youth on the first leg of their journey from humanity to cattle; with storing and feeding and starvation and suffocation and pestilence and death; with slave ship stenches and mutinies of crew and cargo; with the jettying of cargoes before the guns of British cruisers; with auction blocks and sales and profits and losses.

All these words from the seller, but not one word from the sold. The Kings and Captains whose words moved ships. But not one word from the cargo. The thoughts of the "black ivory," the "coin of Africa," had no market value. Africa's ambassadors to the New World have come and worked and died, and left their spoor, but no recorded thought.

Of all the millions transported from Africa to the Americas, only one man is left. He is called Cudjo Lewis and is living at present at Plateau, Alabama, a suburb of Mobile. This is the story of this Cudjo.

I had met Cudjo Lewis for the first time in July 1927. I was sent by Dr. Franz Boas to get a firsthand report of the raid that had brought him to America and bondage, for Dr. Carter G. Woodson of the *Journal of Negro History*. I had talked with him in December of that same year and again in 1928. Thus, from Cudjo and from the records of the Mobile Historical Society, I had the story of the last load of slaves brought into the United States.

The four men responsible for this last deal in human flesh, before the surrender of Lee at Appomattox should end the 364 years of Western slave trading, were the three Meaher brothers and one Captain [William "Bill"] Foster. Jim, Tim, and Burns Meaher were natives of Maine. They had a mill and shipyard on the Alabama River at the mouth of Chickasabogue Creek (now called Three-Mile Creek) where they built swift vessels for blockade running, filibustering expeditions, and river trade. Captain Foster was associated with the Meahers in business. He was "born in Nova Scotia of English parents." . . .

The *Clotilda* was the fastest boat in their possession, and she was the one selected to make the trip. Captain Foster seems to have been the actual owner of the vessel. Perhaps that is the reason he sailed in command. The clearance papers state that she was sailing for the west coast for a cargo of red palm oil. Foster had a crew of Yankee sailors and sailed directly for Whydah [Ouidah], the slave port of Dahomey. . . .

When Captain Foster arrived in May, the wars being just over for the year, he had a large collection to choose from. The people he chose had been in the stockade behind the great white house for less than a month. He selected 130, equal number of men and women, paid for them, got into his hammock and was conveyed across the shallow river to the beach, and was shot through the surf by the skillful Kroo boys and joined his ship. In other boats manipulated by the Kroo boys were his pieces of property.

When 116 of the slaves had been brought aboard, Foster, up in the rigging, observing all the activities of the Port through his glasses, became alarmed. He saw all the Dahoman ships suddenly run up black flags. "He hurried down and gave orders" to abandon the cargo not already on board, and to sail away with all speed. He says that the Dahomans were treacherously planning to recapture the cargo he had just bought and hold him for ransom. But the *Clotilda* was so expertly handled and her speed was so great that she sped away to safety with all ease....

The Africans were kept at Dabney's Place for eleven days: being only allowed to talk "in whispers" and being constantly moved from place to place.

> At the end of the eleventh day clothes were brought to them and they were put aboard the steamer *Commodore* and carried to The Bend in Clark County, where the Alabama and the Tombigbee rivers meet and where Burns Meaher had a plantation.
>
> There they were lodged each night under a wagon shed, and driven each morning before daybreak back into the swamp, where they remained until dark.

"Meaher sent word secretly to those disposed to buy. They were piloted to the place of concealment by Jim Dennison. The Africans were placed in two long rows," men in one row, women in the other. Some couples were bought and taken to Selma. The remainder were divided up among the Meahers and Foster, Captain Jim Meaher took thirty-two (sixteen couples); Captain Burns Meaher took ten Africans; Foster received ten; and Captain Tim Meaher took eight. Finally, after a period of adjustment, the slaves were put to work. Before a year had passed, the war of Secession broke out. With the danger from interference from the Federal Government removed, all the Africans not sold to Selma were brought to the Meaher plantations at Magazine Point....

The village that these Africans built after freedom came, they called "African Town." The town is now called Plateau, Alabama. The new name was bestowed upon it by the Mobile and Birmingham Railroad (now a part of the Southern Railroad System) built through [the town]. But still its dominant tone is African.

With these things already known to me, I once more sought the ancient house of the man called Cudjo. This singular man who says of himself, *"Edem etie ukum edem etie upar"*: The tree of two woods, literally, two trees that have grown together. One part *ukum* (mahogany) and one part *upar* (ebony). He means to say, "Partly a free man, partly free." The only man on earth who has in his heart the memory of his African home; the horrors of a slave raid; the barracoon; the Lenten tones of slavery; and who has sixty-seven years of freedom in a foreign land behind him.

How does one sleep with such memories beneath the pillow? How does a pagan live with a Christian God? How has the Nigerian "heathen" borne up under the process of civilization?

I was sent to ask.

"Political Education Neglected"
from *The Mis-Education of the Negro* (1933)

Carter G. Woodson

Noted writer, journalist, scholar, and historian Carter G. Woodson (1875–1950) published his tour-de-force The Mis-Education of the Negro *in 1933. The text forcefully critiques the US education system and its corrosive effects on Black people through its failure to present authentic and accurate Black histories in schools. Here is an excerpt.*

Some time ago when Congressman Oscar De Priest was distributing by thousands copies of the Constitution of the United States certain wiseacres were disposed to make fun of it. What purpose would such an act serve? These critics, however, probably did not know that thousands and thousands of Negro children in this country are not permitted to use school books in which are printed the Declaration of Independence or the Constitution of the United States. Thomas Jefferson and James Madison are mentioned in their history as figures in politics rather than as expounders of liberty and freedom. These youths are not permitted to learn that Jefferson believed that government should derive its power from the consent of the governed.

Not long ago a measure was introduced in a certain State Legislature to have the Constitution of the United States thus printed in school histories, but when the bill was about to pass it was killed by some one who made the point that it would never do to have Negroes study the Constitution of the United States. If the Negroes were granted the opportunity to peruse this document, they might learn to contend for the rights therein guaranteed; and no Negro teacher who gives attention to such matters of the government is tolerated in those backward districts. The teaching of government or the lack of such instruction, then, must be made to conform to the policy of "keeping the Negro in his place."

In like manner, the teaching of history in the Negro area has had its political significance. Starting out after the Civil War, the opponents of freedom and social justice decided to work out a program which would enslave the Negroes' mind inasmuch as the freedom of body had to be conceded. It was well understood that if by the teaching of history the white man could be further assured of his superiority and the Negro could be made to feel that he had always been a failure and that the subjection of his will to some other race is necessary the freedman, then, would still be a slave. If you can control a man's thinking you do not have to worry about his action. When you determine what a man shall think you do not have to concern yourself about what he will do. If you make a man feel that he is inferior, you do not have to compel him to accept an inferior status, for he will seek it himself. If you make a man think that he is justly an outcast, you do not have to order him to the back door. He will go without being told; and if there is no back door, his very nature will demand one.

This program, so popular immediately after the Civil War, was not new, but after this upheaval, its execution received a new stimulus. Histories written elsewhere for the former slave area were discarded, and new treatments of local and national history in conformity with the recrudescent propaganda were produced to give whites and blacks the biased point of view of the development of the nation and the relations of the races. Special treatments of the Reconstruction period were produced in apparently scientific form by propagandists who went into the first graduate schools of the East to learn modern historiography about half a century ago. Having the stamp of science, the thought of these polemics was accepted in all seats of learning. These rewriters of history fearlessly contended that slavery was a benevolent institution; the masters loved their slaves and treated them humanely; the abolitionists meddled with the institution which the masters eventually would have modified; the Civil War brought about by "fanatics" like William Lloyd Garrison and John Brown was unnecessary; it was a mistake to make the Negro a citizen, for he merely became worse off by incurring the displeasure of the master class that will never tolerate him as an equal; and the Negro must live in this country in a state of recognized inferiority.

"The Propaganda of History"

from *Black Reconstruction in America* (1935)

W. E. B. Du Bois

W. E. B. Du Bois (1868–1963) is perhaps one of the most influential sociologists and well-known advocates of Black freedom throughout the twentieth century. In 1895, Du Bois became the first Black scholar to receive a PhD from Harvard University. He is the author of discipline-setting titles like The Souls of Black Folk *(1903) and* Black Reconstruction in America: Toward a History of the Part Which Black Folk Played in the Attempt to Reconstruct Democracy in America, 1860–1880 *(1935). In "The Propaganda of History"—a chapter from* Black Reconstruction *excerpted below—Du Bois argues that the teaching and learning of history has often served as a tool of propaganda for defenders of the status quo, especially in relation, in this case, to Black history.*

How the facts of American history have in the last half century been falsified because the nation was ashamed. The South was ashamed because it fought to perpetuate human slavery. The North was ashamed because it had to call in the black men to save the Union, abolish slavery and establish democracy.

What are American children taught today about Reconstruction? Helen Boardman has made a study of current textbooks and notes these three dominant theses:

1. *All Negroes were ignorant.*

"All were ignorant of public business." (Woodburn and Moran, "Elementary American History and Government," p. 397.)

"Although the Negroes were now free, they were also ignorant and unfit to govern themselves." (Everett Barnes, "American History for Grammar Grades," p. 334.)

"The Negroes got control of these states. They had been slaves all their lives, and were so ignorant they did not even know the letters of the alphabet. Yet they now sat in the state legislatures and made the laws." (D. H. Montgomery, "The Leading Facts of American History," p. 332.)

"In the South, the Negroes who had so suddenly gained their freedom did not know what to do with it." (Hubert Cornish and Thomas Hughes, "History of the United States for Schools," p. 345.)

"In the legislatures, the Negroes were so ignorant that they could only watch their white leaders—carpetbaggers, and vote aye or no as they were told." (S. E. Forman, "Advanced American History," Revised Edition, p. 452.)

"Some legislatures were made up of a few dishonest white men and several Negroes, many too ignorant to know anything about law-making." (Hubert Cornish and Thomas Hughes, "History of the United States for Schools," p. 349.)

2. *All Negroes were lazy, dishonest and extravagant.*

"These men knew not only nothing about the government, but also cared for nothing except what they could gain for themselves." (Helen F. Giles, "How the United States Became a World Power," p. 7.)

"Legislatures were often at the mercy of Negroes, childishly ignorant, who sold their votes openly, and whose 'loyalty' was gained by allowing them to eat, drink and clothe themselves at the state's expense." (William J. Long, "America—A History of Our Country," p. 392.)

"Some Negroes spent their money foolishly, and were worse off than they had been before." (Carl Russell Fish, "History of America," p. 385.)

"This assistance led many freed men to believe that they need no longer work. They also ignorantly believed that the lands of their former masters were to be turned over by Congress to them, and that every Negro was to have as his allotment 'forty acres and a mule.'" (W. F. Gordy, "History of the United States," Part II, p. 336.)

"Thinking that slavery meant toil and that freedom meant only idleness, the slave after he was set free was disposed to try out his freedom by refusing to work." (S. E. Forman, "Advanced American History," Revised Edition.)

"They began to wander about, stealing and plundering. In one week, in a Georgia town, 150 Negroes were arrested for thieving." (Helen F. Giles, "How the United States Became a World Power," p. 6.)

3. *Negroes were responsible for bad government during Reconstruction.*

"Foolish laws were passed by the black law-makers, the public money was wasted terribly and thousands of dollars were stolen straight. Self-respecting Southerners chafed under the horrible régime." (Emerson David Fite, "These United States," p. 37.)

"In the exhausted states already amply 'punished' by the desolation of war, the rule of the Negro and his unscrupulous carpetbagger and scalawag patrons, was an orgy of extravagance, fraud and disgusting incompetency." (David Saville Muzzey, "History of the American People," p. 408.)

"The picture of Reconstruction which the average pupil in these sixteen States receives is limited to the South. The South found it necessary to pass Black Codes for the control of the shiftless and sometimes vicious freedmen. The Freedmen's Bureau caused the Negroes to look to the North rather than to the South for support and by giving them a false sense of equality did more harm than good. With the scalawags, the ignorant and non-propertyholding Negroes under the leadership of the carpetbaggers, engaged in a wild orgy of spending in the legislatures. The humiliation and distress of the Southern whites was in part relieved by the Ku Klux Klan, a secret organization which frightened the superstitious blacks."

Grounded in such elementary and high school teaching, an American youth attending college today would learn from current textbooks of history that the Constitution recognized slavery; that the chance of getting rid of slavery by peaceful methods was ruined by the Abolitionists; that after the period of Andrew Jackson, the two sections of the United States "had become fully conscious of their conflicting interests. Two irreconcilable forms of civilization . . . in the North, the democratic . . . in the South, a more stationary and aristocratic civilization." He would read that Harriet Beecher Stowe brought on the Civil War; that the assault on Charles Sumner was due to his "coarse invective" against a South Carolina Senator; and that Negroes were the only people to achieve emancipation with no effort on their part. That Reconstruction was a disgraceful attempt to subject white people to ignorant Negro rule;

and that, according to a Harvard professor of history (the italics are ours), "Legislative expenses were grotesquely extravagant; the *colored members in some states engaging in a saturnalia of corrupt expenditure*" (Encyclopaedia Britannica, 14th Edition, Volume 22, p. 815, by Frederick Jackson Turner).

In other words, he would in all probability complete his education without any idea of the part which the black race has played in America; of the tremendous moral problem of abolition; of the cause and meaning of the Civil War and the relation which Reconstruction had to democratic government and the labor movement today.

Herein lies more than mere omission and difference of emphasis. The treatment of the period of Reconstruction reflects small credit upon American historians as scientists. We have too often a deliberate attempt so to change the facts of history that the story will make pleasant reading for Americans. . . .

"The San Domingo Masses Begin"
from *The Black Jacobins* (1938)

C. L. R. James

Born in Trinidad, C. L. R. James (1901–1989) was a cultural historian and leader in the twentieth-century Pan-African movement. Known as a prolific writer and astute political thinker, he published The Black Jacobins: Toussaint L'Ouverture and the San Domingo Revolution— *his systematic study of the Haitian Revolution—in 1938. In the excerpt that follows, James critiques the ability of liberal reform to produce the outcome of Black freedom.*

But what of the slaves? The slaves had revolted for freedom. The revolt was to be suppressed. But at least there might be a promise of pardon, of kind treatment in the future. Not a word. Neither from Vaublanc on the Right nor Robespierre on the Left. Robespierre made an ass of himself by violently objecting to the word slavery, when proposed as a substitute for non-free. Brissot made a passing reference to them as being unfortunate, and that was all.

"The cause of the men of colour is then the cause of the patriots of the old Third Estate and finally of the people so long oppressed." So had spoken Brissot, and Brissot, representative of the Third Estate, was prepared to help the Third Estate of the Mulattoes and give the people, in France as well as in San Domingo, phrases. The French peasants were still clamouring for the Assembly to relieve them of the feudal dues. The Brissotins would not do it. They would not touch property, and the slaves were property. Blangetty, a deputy, proposed a motion for gradual enfranchisement. The Legislative would not even discuss it. On March 26th, two days after the decree in favour of the Mulattoes, Ducos dared to propose that every Mulatto child be free, "whatever the status of its mother." The Legislative in wrath voted the previous question, and Ducos was not even allowed to speak on his motion. The Friends of the Negro, good Liberals, were now in power and were as silent about slavery as any colonist. The slaves, ignorant of politics, had been right not to wait on these eloquent phrase-makers. Toussaint, that astute student of French politics, read and noted.

Toussaint alone among the black leaders, with freedom for all in his mind, was in those early months of 1792 organising out of the thousands of ignorant and untrained blacks an army capable of fighting European troops. The insurgents had developed a method of attack based on their overwhelming numerical superiority. They did not rush forward in mass formation like fanatics. They placed themselves in groups, choosing wooded spots in such a way as to envelop their enemy, seeking to crush him by weight of numbers. They carried out these preliminary manoeuvres in dead silence, while their priests (the black ones) chanted the wanga, and the women and children sang and danced in a frenzy. When these had reached the necessary height of excitement the fighters attacked. If they met with resistance, they retired without exhausting themselves, but at the slightest hesitation in the defence they became extremely bold and, rushing up to the cannon, swarmed all over their opponents. At first they could not even use the guns they captured, and used to apply the match at the wrong end. It was from these men "unable to speak two words of French" that an army had to be made. Toussaint could have had thousands following him. It is characteristic of him that he began with a few hundred picked men, devoted to himself, who learnt the art of war with him from the beginning, as they fought side by side against the French troops and the colonists. In camp he drilled and trained them assiduously. By July 1792, he had no more than five hundred attached to himself, the best of the revolutionary troops. These and not the perorations in the Legislative would be decisive in the struggle for freedom. But nobody took much notice of Toussaint and his black followers. Feuillants and Jacobins in France, whites and Mulattoes in San Domingo, were still looking upon the slave revolt as a huge riot which would be put down in time, once the division between the slave-owners was closed.

"The Origin of Negro Slavery"
from *Capitalism and Slavery* (1944)

Eric Williams

*Educator, historian, philosopher, and former prime minister of Trinidad
and Tobago, Eric Williams (1911–1981) was a prolific scholar whose
work explores the political economy of race in the Caribbean and beyond.
Published in 1944, his well-known* Capitalism and Slavery *examines
slavery's elemental role in the development of British capitalism and
argues that transatlantic trade and plantation slavery made industrial-
ization in England possible. In the excerpt below, Williams argues that
the ideology of race grew out of slavery (and not the opposite, as many
assume) to rationalize the centrality of its economic exploitation.*

Here, then, is the origin of Negro slavery. The reason was economic, not racial;
it had to do not with the color of the laborer, but the cheapness of the labor. As
compared with Indian and white labor, Negro slavery was eminently superior.
"In each case," writes Bassett, discussing North Carolina, "it was a survival of
the fittest. Both Indian slavery and white servitude were to go down before the
black man's superior endurance, docility, and labor capacity." The features of
the man, his hair, color and dentifrice, his "subhuman" characteristics so widely pleaded, were only the later rationalizations to justify a simple economic
fact: that the colonies needed labor and resorted to Negro labor because it was
cheapest and best. This was not a theory, it was a practical conclusion deduced
from the personal experience of the planter. He would have gone to the moon, if

necessary, for labor. Africa was nearer than the moon, nearer too than the more populous countries of India and China. But their turn was to come.

This white servitude is of cardinal importance for an understanding of the development of the New World and the Negro's place in that development. It completely explodes the old myth that the whites could not stand the strain of manual labor in the climate of the New World and that, for this reason and this reason alone, the European powers had recourse to Africans. The argument is quite untenable. A Mississippi dictum will have it that "only black men and mules can face the sun in July." But the whites faced the sun for well over a hundred years in Barbados, and the Salzburgers of Georgia indignantly denied that rice cultivation was harmful to them. The Caribbean islands are well within the tropical zone, but their climate is more equable than tropical, the temperature rarely exceeds 80 degrees though it remains uniform the whole year round, and they are exposed to the gentle winds from the sea. The unbearable humidity of an August day in some parts of the United States has no equal in the islands. Moreover only the southern tip of Florida in the United States is actually tropical, yet Negro labor flourished in Virginia and Carolina. The southern parts of the United States are not hotter than South Italy or Spain, and de Tocqueville asked why the European could not work there as well as in those two countries? When Whitney invented his cotton gin, it was confidently expected that cotton would be produced by free labor on small farms, and it was, in fact, so produced. Where the white farmer was ousted, the enemy was not the climate but the slave plantation, and the white farmer moved westward, until the expanding plantation sent him on his wanderings again. Writing in 1857, Weston pointed out that labor in the fields of the extreme South and all the heavy outdoor work in New Orleans were performed by whites, without any ill consequences. "No part of the continental borders of the Gulf of Mexico," he wrote, "and none of the islands which separate it from the ocean, need be abandoned to the barbarism of negro slavery." In our own time we who have witnessed the dispossession of Negroes by white sharecroppers in the South and the mass migration of Negroes from the South to the colder climates of Detroit, New York, Pittsburgh and other industrial centers of the North, can no longer accept the convenient rationalization that Negro labor was employed on the slave plantations because the climate was too rigorous for the constitution of the white man.

A constant and steady emigration of poor whites from Spain to Cuba, to the very end of Spanish dominion, characterized Spanish colonial policy. Fernando Ortíz has drawn a striking contrast between the role of tobacco and sugar in Cuban history. Tobacco was a free white industry intensively cultivated on small farms; sugar was a black slave industry extensively cultivated on large plantations. He further compared the free Cuban tobacco industry with its slave Virginian counterpart. What determined the difference was not climate but the economic structure of the two areas. The whites could hardly have endured the tropical heat of Cuba and succumbed to the tropical heat of Barbados. In Puerto Rico, the jíbaro, the poor white peasant, is still the basic type, demonstrating, in the words of Grenfell Price, how erroneous is the belief that after three generations the white man cannot breed in the tropics. Similar white communities have survived in the Caribbean, from the earliest settlements right down to our own times, in the Dutch West Indian islands of Saba and St. Martin. For some sixty years French settlers have lived in St. Thomas not only as fishermen but as agriculturalists, forming today the "largest single farming class" in the island. As Dr. Price concludes: "It appears that northern whites can retain a fair standard for generations in the trade-wind tropics if the location is free from the worst forms of tropical disease, if the economic return is adequate, and if the community is prepared to undertake hard, physical work." Over one hundred years ago a number of German emigrants settled in Seaford, Jamaica. They survive today, with no visible signs of deterioration, flatly contradicting the popular belief as to the possibility of survival of the northern white in the tropics. Wherever, in short, tropical agriculture remained on a small farming basis, whites not only survived but prospered. Where the whites disappeared, the cause was not the climate but the supersession of the small farm by the large plantation, with its consequent demand for a large and steady supply of labor.

The climatic theory of the plantation is thus nothing but a rationalization. In an excellent essay on the subject Professor Edgar Thompson writes: "The plantation is not to be accounted for by climate. It is a political institution." It is, we might add, more: it is an economic institution. The climatic theory "is part of an ideology which rationalizes and naturalizes an existing social and economic order, and this everywhere seems to be an order in which there is a race problem."

"A Talk to Teachers" (October 16, 1963)

James Baldwin

*As an essayist and novelist, James Baldwin (1924–1987) explored the
condition of Black life in the US and abroad. Known for his wit and phil-
osophical acumen, he used his literary talents to support Black freedom
movements throughout the twentieth century and to explore themes such
as race, gender, queerness, religion, and beyond. In the following excerpt
from his "Talk to Teachers," Baldwin lays out the fundamental purposes
of education as they relate to Black liberation and racial justice.*

The paradox of education is precisely this—that as one begins to become conscious one begins to examine the society in which he is being educated. The
purpose of education, finally, is to create in a person the ability to look at the
world for himself, to make his own decisions, to say to himself this is black or
this is white, to decide for himself whether there is a God in heaven or not. To
ask questions of the universe, and then learn to live with those questions, is the
way he achieves his own identity. But no society is really anxious to have that
kind of person around. What societies really, ideally, want is a citizenry which
will simply obey the rules of society. If a society succeeds in this, that society is
about to perish. The obligation of anyone who thinks of himself as responsible
is to examine society and try to change it and to fight it—at no matter what risk.
This is the only hope society has. This is the only way societies change.

    Now, if what I have tried to sketch has any validity, it becomes thoroughly
clear, at least to me, that any Negro who is born in this country and undergoes
the American educational system runs the risk of becoming schizophrenic. On

the one hand he is born in the shadow of the stars and stripes and he is assured
it represents a nation which has never lost a war. He pledges allegiance to that
flag which guarantees "liberty and justice for all." He is part of a country in
which anyone can become President, and so forth. But on the other hand he
is also assured by his country and his countrymen that he has never contributed anything to civilization—that his past is nothing more than a record of
humiliations gladly endured. He is assumed by the republic that he, his father,
his mother, and his ancestors were happy, shiftless, watermelon-eating darkies
who loved Mr. Charlie and Miss Ann, that the value he has as a black man is
proven by one thing only—his devotion to white people. If you think I am exag-
gerating, examine the myths which proliferate in this country about Negroes.

Now, all this enters the child's consciousness much sooner than we as
adults would like to think it does. As adults, we are easily fooled because we are
so anxious to be fooled. But children are very different. Children, not yet aware
that it is dangerous to look too deeply at anything, look at everything, look at
each other, and draw their own conclusions. They don't have the vocabulary
to express what they see, and we, their elders, know how to intimidate them
very easily and very soon. But a black child, looking at the world around him,
though he cannot know quite what to make of it, is aware that there is a reason
why his mother works so hard, why his father is always on edge. He is aware
that there is some reason why, if he sits down in the front of the bus, his father or
mother slaps him and drags him to the back of the bus. He is aware that there is
some terrible weight on his parents' shoulders which menaces him. And it isn't
long—in fact it begins when he is in school—before he discovers the shape of
his oppression. . . .

I began by saying that one of the paradoxes of education was that precisely
at the point when you begin to develop a conscience, you must find yourself at
war with your society. It is your responsibility to change society if you think of
yourself as an educated person. And on the basis of the evidence—the moral
and political evidence—one is compelled to say that this is a backward society.
Now if I were a teacher in this school, or any Negro school, and I was dealing
with Negro children, who were in my care only a few hours of every day and
would then return to their homes and to the streets, children who have an ap-
prehension of their future which with every hour grows grimmer and darker, I
would try to teach them—I would try to make them know—that those streets,

those houses, those dangers, those agonies by which they are surrounded, are
criminal. I would try to make each child know that these things are the result
of a criminal conspiracy to destroy him. I would teach him that if he intends to
get to be a man, he must at once decide that his is stronger than this conspiracy
and that he must never make his peace with it. And that one of his weapons for
refusing to make his peace with it and for destroying it depends on what he de-
cides he is worth. I would teach him that there are currently very few standards
in this country which are worth a man's respect. That it is up to him to begin to
change these standards for the sake of the life and the health of the country. I
would suggest to him that the popular culture—as represented, for example,
on television and in comic books and in movies—is based on fantasies created
by very ill people, and he must be aware that these are fantasies that have nothing to do with reality. I would teach him that the press he reads is not as free as
it says it is—and that he can do something about that, too. I would try to make
him know that just as American history is longer, larger, more various, more
beautiful, and more terrible than anything anyone has ever said about it, so is
the world larger, more daring, more beautiful and more terrible, but principally
larger—and that it belongs to him. I would teach him that he doesn't have to be
bound by the expediencies of any given Administration, any given policy, any
given time—that he has the right and the necessity to examine everything. . . .

Black Panther Party "Ten-Point Program" (1966)

Huey Newton and Bobby Seale

In 1966, Bobby Seale and Huey Newton (1942–1989) drafted one of the most well-known political documents of the twentieth century, "What We Want Now! What We Believe," also known as the Black Panther Party's Ten-Point Program, at the time of the party's founding in Oakland, California. This document lays out a vision and a blueprint for Black liberation through the lenses of self-defense and social support.

To those poor souls who don't know Black history, the beliefs and desires of the Black Panther Party for Self Defense may seem unreasonable. To Black people, the ten points covered are absolutely essential to survival. We have listened to the riot producing words "these things take time" for 400 years. The Black Panther Party knows what Black people want and need. Black unity and self defense will make these demands a reality.

WHAT WE WANT

1. We want freedom. We want power to determine the destiny of our Black community.
2. We want full employment for our people.
3. We want an end to the robbery by the White man of our Black community.
4. We want decent housing, fit for shelter [of] human beings.
5. We want education for our people that exposes the true nature of

this decadent American society. We want education that teaches us our true history and our role in the present day society.

6. We want all Black men to be exempt from military service.

7. We want an immediate end to police brutality and murder of Black people.

8. We want freedom for all Black men held in federal, state, county, and city prisons and jails.

9. We want all Black people when brought to trial to be tried in court by a jury of their peer group or people from their Black communities. As defined by the constitution of the United States.

10. We want land, bread, housing, education, clothing, justice and peace.

WHAT WE BELIEVE

1. We believe that Black people will not be free until we are able to determine our destiny.

2. We believe that the federal government is responsible and obligated to give every man employment or a guaranteed income. We believe that if the White American business men will not give full employment, then the means of production should be taken from the business men and placed in the community so that the people of the community can organize and employ all of its people and give a high standard of living.

3. We believe that this racist government has robbed us and now we are demanding the overdue debt of forty acres and two mules. Forty acres and two mules was promised 100 years ago as retribution for slave labor and mass murder of Black people. We will accept the payment in currency which will be distributed to our many communities: the Germans are now aiding the Jews in Israel for the genocide of the Jewish people. The Germans murdered 6,000,000 Jews. The American racist has taken part in the slaughter of over 50,000,000 Black people; therefore, we feel that this is a modest demand that we make.

4. We believe that if the White landlords will not give decent housing to our Black community, then the housing and the land should be made into cooperatives so that our community, with government

aid, can build and make decent housing for its people.

5. We believe in an educational system that will give to our people a knowledge of self. If a man does not have knowledge of himself and his position in society and the world, then he has little chance to relate to anything else.

6. We believe that Black people should not be forced to fight in the military service to defend a racist government that does not protect us. We will not fight and kill other people of color in the world who, like Black people, are being victimized by the White racist government of America. We will protect ourselves from the force and violence of the racist police and the racist military, by whatever means necessary.

7. We believe we can end police brutality in our Black community by organizing Black self defense groups that are dedicated to defending our Black community from racist police oppression and brutality. The Second Amendment of the Constitution of the United States gives us a right to bear arms. We therefore believe that all Black people should arm themselves for self defense.

8. We believe that all Black people should be released from the many jails and prisons because they have not received a fair and impartial trial.

9. We believe that the courts should follow the United States Constitution so that Black people will receive fair trials. The 14th amendment of the U.S. Constitution gives a man a right to be tried by his peer group. A peer is a person from a similar economic, social, religious, geographical, environmental, historical and racial background. To do this the court will be forced to select a jury from the Black community from which the Black defendant came. We have been, and are being tried by all White juries that have no understanding of the "average reasoning man" of the Black community.

10. When in the course of human events, it becomes necessary for one people to dissolve the political bonds which have connected them with another, and to assume among the powers of the earth, the separate and equal station to which the laws of nature and nature's god entitle them, a decent respect to the opinions of mankind requires that they should declare the causes which impel them to separation. We hold these truths to be self-evident, that all men are created

equal, that they are endowed by their creator with certain inalienable rights, that among these are life, liberty and the pursuit of happiness. That to secure these rights, governments are instituted among men, deriving their just powers from the consent of the governed,—that whenever any form of government becomes destructive of these ends, it is the right of people to alter or to abolish it, and to institute new government, laying its foundation on such principles and organizing its powers in such form as to them shall seem most likely to effect their safety and happiness. Prudence, indeed, will dictate that governments long established should not be changed for light and transient causes; and accordingly all experience hath shewn, that mankind are more disposed to suffer, while evils are sufferable, than to right themselves by abolishing the forms to which they are accustomed. But when a long train of abuses and usurpations, pursuing invariably the same object, evinces a design to reduce them under absolute despotism, it is their right, it is their duty, to throw off such government, and to provide new guards for their future security.

"Double Jeopardy: To Be Black and Female" from *Black Women's Manifesto* (1969)

Frances Beal

Black feminist thinker and activist Frances Beal was a founding member of SNCC's Black Women's Liberation Committee. She is well known for cocreating Black Women's Manifesto, *an influential political pamphlet that critiques the intersected outcomes of capitalism and patriarchy, and offers an affirmative vision for the role of Black women in the revolution. An excerpt follows.*

The black community and black women especially, must begin raising questions about the kind of society we wish to see established. We must note the ways in which capitalism oppresses us and then move to create institutions that will eliminate these destructive influences.

The new world that we are struggling to create must destroy oppression of any type. The value of this new system will be determined by the status of those persons who are presently most oppressed—the low man on the totem pole. Unless women in any enslaved nation are completely liberated, the change cannot really be called a revolution. If the black woman has to retreat to the position she occupied before the armed struggle, the whole movement and the whole struggle will have retreated in terms of truly freeing the colonized population.

A people's revolution that engages the participation of every member of the community, including men, and women, brings about a certain transformation in the participants as a result of this participation. Once you have caught a glimpse of freedom or tasted a bit of self-determination, you can't go back to old routines that were established under a racist, capitalist regime. We must begin to understand that a revolution entails not only the willingness to lay our lives on the firing line and get killed. In some ways, this is an easy commitment to make. To die for the revolution is a oneshot deal; to live for the revolution means taking on the more difficult commitment of changing our day-to-day life patterns.

This will mean changing the traditional routines that we have established as a result of living in a totally corrupting society. It means changing how you relate to your wife, your husband, your parents and your coworkers. If we are going to liberate ourselves as a people, it must be recognized that black women have very specific problems that have to be spoken to. We must be liberated along with the rest of the population. We cannot wait to start working on those problems until that great day in the future when the revolution somehow miraculously, is accomplished.

To assign women the role of housekeeper and mother while men go forth into battle is a highly questionable doctrine for a revolutionary to profess. Each individual must develop a high political consciousness in order to understand how this system enslaves us all and what actions we must take to bring about its total destruction. Those who consider themselves to be revolutionary must begin to deal with other revolutionaries as equals. And so far as I know, revolutionaries are not determined by sex.

Old people, young people, men and women must take part in the struggle. To relegate women to purely supportive roles or to simply cultural considerations is dangerous doctrine to project. Unless black men who are preparing themselves for armed struggle understand that the society which we are trying to create is one in which the oppression of ALL MEMBERS of that society is eliminated, then the revolution will have failed in its avowed Purpose.

Given the mutual commitment of black men and black women alike to the liberation of our people and other oppressed peoples around the world, the total involvement of each individual is necessary. A revolutionary has the responsibility of not only toppling those that are now in a position of power, but more importantly, the responsibility of creating new institutions that will eliminate all forms of oppression for all people. We must begin to rewrite our understanding of traditional personal relationships between man and woman.

All the resources that the black community can muster up must be channeled into the struggle. Black women must take an active part in bringing about the kind of world where our children, our loved ones, and each citizen can grow up and live as decent human beings, free from the pressures of racism and capitalist exploitation.

"Black Studies: Bringing Back the Person" (1969)

June Jordan

*Acclaimed poet, journalist, educator, and essayist June Jordan (1936–
2002) was known for her wide-ranging social critique and commentary
in the areas of feminism, LGBTQ+ rights, and Black freedom. The
excerpt that follows is from Jordan's "Black Studies: Bringing Back the
Person," which eloquently argues that the Eurocentrism of US universities must be uprooted if they are to be of any use to Black students and in
challenging the racist status quo.*

... We choose community: Black America, in white. Here we began like objects
chosen by the blind. And it is here that we see fit to continue—as subjects of
human community. We will to bring back the person, alive and sacrosanct; we
mean to rescue the person from the amorality of time and science.

History prepares the poor, the victims of unnecessary injustice, to spit at
tradition, to blow up the laboratories, to despise all knowledge recklessly loos-
ened from the celebration of all human life. And still, it lies there, the university
campus, frequently green, and signifying power: power to the people who feed
their egos on the grass, inside the gates.

Black American history prepares Black students to seize possibilities of
power even while they tremble about purpose. *Efficiency, competence*: Black
students know the deadly, neutral definition of these words. There seldom has
been a more efficient system for profiteering, through human debasement,
than the plantations, of a while ago. Today, the whole world sits, as quietly
scared as it can sit, afraid that, tomorrow, America may direct its efficiency

and competence toward another forest for defoliation, or clean-cut laser-beam extermination.

Black American history prepares Black people to believe that true history is hidden and destroyed, or that history results from a logical bundling of lies that mutilate and kill. We have been prepared, by our American experience, to believe that civilization festers between opposite poles of plunder and pain. And still, the university waits, unavoidable, at the end of compulsory education, to assure the undisturbed perpetuity of this civilization. . . .

There has been no choosing until now. Until the university, there is no choice. Education is compulsory. Education has paralleled the history of our Black lives; it has been characterized by the punishment of nonconformity, abridgment, withered enthusiasm, distortion, and self-denying censorship. Education has paralleled the life of prospering white America; it has been characterized by reverence for efficiency, cultivation of competence unattended by concern for aim, big white lies, and the mainly successful blackout of Black life.

Black students arrive at the university from somewhere. Where is that, exactly? Where is Black America, all of it, from the beginning? Why do we ask? How does it happen that we do not know?

What is the university, until we arrive? Is it where the teachers of children receive their training? It is where the powerful become more powerful. It is where the norms of this abnormal power, this America, receive the ultimate worship of propagation. It is where the people become usable parts of the whole machine: Machine is not community.

"Toward a Black Psychology" (1970)

Joseph White

Joseph L. White is known as the "Godfather of Black Psychology" and cofounded the Association of Black Psychologists in 1968. In "Toward a Black Psychology," which appeared in Ebony *magazine, he explains why a strength-based approach is necessary when describing the mental wellness of Black Americans. He argues that no perspective, theory, or rationale based in Eurocentrism can accurately understand Black mental health when the (white) mainstream foundations of psychology assume Black people to be inadequate. White posits that Black people must define their own power and also create the tools by which power is measured in the first place.*

Regardless of what black people ultimately decide about the questions of separation, integration, segregation, revolution or reform, it is vitally important that we develop, out of the authentic experience of black people in this country, an accurate workable theory of black psychology. It is very difficult, if not impossible, to understand the life styles of black people using traditional theories developed by white psychologists to explain white people. Moreover, when these traditional theories are applied to the lives of black folks many incorrect, weakness-dominated and inferiority oriented conclusions come about.

In all fairness it should be said that only a few white psychologists publicly accept the idea most recently advanced by Dr. Jensen (see Carl Rowan's review of Jensen's work in the May issue of *Ebony Magazine*) that black people, according to his research findings, are at birth genetically inferior to whites in intellectual potential. Most psychologists and social scientists take the more liberal point of view which in essence states that black people are culturally deprived and psychologically maladjusted because the environment in which they were reared as children and in which continue to rear their own children lacks the necessary early experiences to prepare us for excellence in school, appropriate sex role behavior and, generally speaking, achievement within an Anglo middle class frame of reference. In short, we are culturally and psychologically deprived because our experiential background provides us with inferior preparation to move effectively within the dominant white culture.

A simple journey with the white researcher into the black home may provide us with some insight into how such important, but somewhat erroneous, conclusions are reached. During this visit to the black home the researcher may not find familiar aspects of the white culture such as Book-of-the-Month selections, records of Broadway plays, classics, magazines such as *Harpers*, the *Atlantic Monthly* or the *New York Review of Books*. He might also observe a high noise level, continuously reinforced by inputs from blues and rhythm radio stations, TV programs and several sets of conversations going on at once. This type of observation leads him to assume that the homes of black children are very weak in intellectual content, uninteresting and generally confusing places to grow up. Somehow he fails to see the intellectual stimulation that might be provided by local black newspapers, informative rapping, *Jet, Ebony*, Sepia and the Motown sound. Black children in these same homes who supposedly can't read (even preschoolers) can sing several rock and blues tunes from memory and correctly identify the songs of popular entertainers. These same researchers or educational psychologists listening to black speech assume that our use of non-standard oral English is an example of bad grammar without recognizing the possibility that we have a valid, legitimate, alternate dialect.

As the white educational psychologist continues with what for him has become a standard analysis, the next step becomes one of setting up programs which provide black children with the kind of enrichment he feels is needed to overcome and compensate for their cultural deprivation. As a consequence of this type of thinking, in recent years from Headstart, New Horizons to Upward Bound, we have repeatedly witnessed the failure of compensatory and enrichment educational programs. Possibly, if social scientists, psychologists and educators would stop trying to compensate for the so-called weaknesses of the black child and try to develop a theory that capitalizes on his strengths, programs could be designed which from the get-go might be more productive and successful.

Many of these same so-called culturally deprived youngsters have developed the kind of mental toughness and survival skills, in terms of coping with life, which make them in many ways superior to their white age-mates who are growing up in the material affluence of Little League suburbias. These black youngsters know how to deal effectively with bill collectors, building superintendents, corner grocery stores, hypes, pimps, whores, sickness and death. They know how to jive school counselors, principals, teachers, welfare workers, juvenile authorities, and in doing so, display a lot of psychological cleverness and originality. They recognize very early that they exist in an environment which is sometimes both complicated and hostile. They may not be able to verbalize it but they have already mastered what existential psychologists state to be the basic human condition; namely that in this life, pain and struggle are unavoidable and that a complete sense of one's identity can only be achieved by both recognizing and directly confronting an unkind and alien existence.

Reflections on the Black Woman's Role in the Community of Slaves (1971)

Angela Davis

Angela Y. Davis is a scholar, activist, and writer. Her work as an educa-tor—both at the university level and in the larger public sphere—has always emphasized the importance of building communities of struggle for economic, racial, and gender justice. In the passage from Reflections on the Black Woman's Role in the Community of Slaves *excerpted below, Davis underscores the centrality of Black women in resisting enslavement, organizing for freedom, and defining their humanity by and for themselves.*

Throughout the South (in South and North Carolina, Virginia, Louisiana, Flor-ida, Georgia, Mississippi and Alabama), maroon communities consisting of fu-gitive slaves and their descendants were "an ever present feature"—from 1642 to 1864—of slavery. They provided ". . . havens for fugitives, served as bases for marauding expeditions against nearby plantations and, at times, supplied lead-ership to planned uprisings."

Every detail of these communities was invariably determined by and steeped in resistance, for their raison d'être emanated from their perpetual assault on slavery. Only in a fighting stance could the maroons hope to secure their constantly imperiled freedom. As a matter of necessity, the women of those communities were compelled to define themselves—no less than the men—through their many acts of resistance. Hence, throughout this brief survey the counter-attacks and heroic efforts at defense assisted by maroon women will be a recurring motif.

As it will be seen, black women often poisoned the food and set fire to the houses of their masters. For those who were also employed as domestics these particular overt forms of resistance were especially available.

The vast majority of the incidents to be related involve either tactically unsuccessful assaults or eventually thwarted attempts at defense. In all likelihood, numerous successes were achieved, even against the formidable obstacles posed by the slave system. Many of these were probably unpublicized even at the time of their occurrence, lest they provide encouragement to the rebellious proclivities of other slaves and, for other slaveholders, an occasion for fear and despair.

During the early years of the slave era (1708) a rebellion broke out in New York. Among its participants were surely many women, for one, along with three men, was executed in retaliation for the killing of seven whites. It may not be entirely insignificant that while the men were hanged, she was heinously burned alive. In the same colony, women played an active role in a 1712 uprising in the course of which slaves, with their guns, clubs and knives, killed members of the slaveholding class and managed to wound others. While some of the insurgents—among them a pregnant woman—were captured, others— including a woman—committed suicide rather than surrender.

"In New Orleans one day in 1730 a woman slave received 'a violent blow from a French soldier for refusing to obey him' and in her anger shouted 'that the French should not long insult Negroes.'" As it was later disclosed, she and undoubtedly many other women, had joined in a vast plan to destroy slaveholders. Along with eight men, this dauntless woman was executed. Two years later, Louisiana pronounced a woman and four men leaders of a planned rebellion. They were all executed and, in a typically savage gesture, their heads publicly displayed on poles.

Charleston, South Carolina condemned a black woman to die in 1740 for arson, a form of sabotage, as earlier noted, frequently carried out by women. In Maryland, for instance, a slave woman was executed in 1776 for having destroyed by fire her master's house, his outhouses and tobacco house.

In the thick of the Colonies' war with England, a group of defiant slave women and men were arrested in Saint Andrew's Parish, Georgia in 1774. But before they were captured, they had already brought a number of slave owners to their death.

The maroon communities have been briefly described; from 1782 to 1784, Louisiana was a constant target of maroon attacks. When twenty-five of this community's members were finally taken prisoner, men and women alike were all severely punished.

As can be inferred from previous example, the North did not escape the tremendous impact of fighting black women. In Albany, New York, two women were among three slaves executed for anti-slavery activities in 1794. The respect and admiration accorded the black woman fighter by her people is strikingly illustrated by an incident which transpired in York, Pennsylvania: when, during the early months of 1803, Margaret Bradley was convicted of attempting to poison two white people, the black inhabitants of the area revolted en masse.

> They made several attempts to destroy the town by fire and succeeded, within a period of three weeks, in burning eleven buildings. Patrols were established, strong guards set up, the militia dispatched to the scene of the unrest . . . and a reward of three hundred dollars offered for the capture of the insurrectionists.

A successful elimination by poisoning of several "of our respectable men" (said a letter to the governor of North Carolina) was met by the execution of four or five slaves. One was a woman who was burned alive. In 1810, two women and a man were accused of arson in Virginia. . . .

An intricate and savage web of oppression intruded at every moment into the black woman's life during slavery. Yet a single theme appears at every juncture: the woman transcending, refusing, fighting back, asserting herself over and against terrifying obstacles. It was not her comrade brother against whom her incredible strength was directed. She fought alongside her man, accepting or providing guidance according to her talents and the nature of their tasks. She was in no sense an authoritarian figure; neither her domestic role nor her acts of resistance could relegate the man to the shadows. On the contrary, she herself had just been forced to leave behind the shadowy realm of female passivity in order to assume her rightful place beside the insurgent male.

This portrait cannot, of course, presume to represent every individual slave woman. It is rather a portrait of the potentials and possibilities inherent in the situation to which slave women were anchored. Invariably there were those who did not realize this potential. There were those who were indifferent and a few who were outright traitors. But certainly they were not the vast majority. The image of black women enchaining their men, cultivating relationships with the oppressor is a cruel fabrication which must be called by its right name. It is a dastardly ideological weapon designed to impair our capacity for resistance today by foisting upon us the ideal of male supremacy.

"Politics of the Attack on Black Studies" (1974)

Robert Allen

Robert Allen's scholarship, thinking, and teaching focus on social movements, labor studies, and Black liberation. He is perhaps most well known for his magnum opus Black Awakening in Capitalist America *(1969), in which he argues against the rising tide of Black capitalism as a legitimate tool of Black freedom and justice. In his short essay "Politics of the Attack on Black Studies" excerpted below, Allen illuminates the birth of the field as grounded in political struggle against the forces of white supremacy in US universities and the country writ large.*

The demand for Black Studies cannot be separated from the rise of the militant black student movement in the 1960s. In fact, it is no exaggeration to say that the establishment of hundreds of Black Studies curricula in colleges and universities across the land was a major achievement of the black student movement. This is not to suggest that there was no black educational thrust before 1960. On the contrary, access to higher education has always been a central concern of black activism. Almost a century and a half ago the necessity for education was debated at a series of national black conventions. Later, the founding of black colleges, although made possible by white philanthropy, represented a continuation of black interest in education, as did the turn-of-the-century debate between Booker T. Washington and W. E. B. Du Bois over whether industrial training or academic education should be given priority in the black struggle for equality. Thus, the demand for Black Studies was not so much a sudden departure as it was a variation in a traditional theme within the black movement.

What was new about the 1960s was that (1) for the first time masses of black students became involved in the struggle for educational change, and (2) it was widely recognized that not only were black students and teachers largely excluded from American higher education but the totality of the black experience was not to be found in the curricula of the vast majority of colleges and universities. It was these two factors that led to the demand for Black Studies departments as vehicles for incorporating black people and the black experience into American higher education. (Black colleges did not escape the scrutiny of militant students. These schools were accused of being white colleges in blackface, and courses in black history, literature and art were demanded, along with a demand that the black colleges must "relate" to the local black community.)

The demand for Black Studies was therefore in essence democratic and even integrationist, although it took a form that was superficially separatist. It was a response to educational racism—the virtual exclusion of black people and the black experience from higher education in the United States. By demanding open admission of black students and the establishment of separate Black Studies departments the student activists and their adult supporters were in effect calling for group or collective integration into higher education rather than token integration of a few selected black individuals. This was certainly a militant demand but not revolutionary, since at its core it simply called for a widening of American democracy not the institution of a totally new educational or social order. However, by widening educational democracy Black Studies could pave the way for the introduction of new and revolutionary ideas into the curriculum, and this was correctly perceived as a threat by conservative administrators and faculty.

In the early 1960s, with the culmination of the student sit-in movement in the South, black students began turning their attention to the black college campuses which had served—reluctantly—as their bases of operations. The students' political experience in confronting the white power structure led them to question the political function of black colleges in particular, and higher education in general. They began to understand that despite all the talk about developing a critical intellect, higher education in practice served also to inculcate bourgeois cultural values and behavior patterns and to channel young people into professional slots in the economy. In short, higher education served to strengthen and conserve the prevailing social order. To the young black students, having just done battle with the racism of the downtown businessmen (guardians of the prevailing social order), this realization came as an affront to their newly awakened black consciousness. On black campuses, students and militant teachers began demanding not only curriculum changes but a restructuring and reorientation of the colleges themselves. The student activists moved to turn black college campuses into political bases for organizing the surrounding black communities. To this end they wanted classrooms and other school facilities made available for community use.

In the spring and fall of 1968, the black student rebellion spread to predominantly white campuses in the North and West. At Columbia, Cornell, San Francisco State and countless other schools a familiar scenario was repeated. Students would go on strike (sometimes occupying buildings) and present the administration with a list of demands (sometimes "non-negotiable") that usually included a demand for admission of more black students, hiring of more black faculty, and initiation of a Black Studies curriculum. The fad word of the period was "relevant" (sometimes "revelant"), and it was believed that these demands would make the university relevant to the struggle for liberation, or at least prevent it from remaining an accomplice in racial oppression.

Almost overnight these demands were taken up by other black students, Third World students and sympathetic white students on campus after campus. The outcome (after hundreds of arrests and much head-busting) was a virtual tidal wave of new courses, programs and departments. No school wanted to be the target of demonstrations and disruptive strikes, especially in the face of demands that were generally just (although many administrators were offended by the expletives that usually were not deleted). But the hastiness with which many of the new programs were patched together suggested that they were being offered as palliatives, or pacification programs to cool out the students, rather than as serious innovations in the educational process. Some schools simply took all their courses touching upon race relations and minority groups, lumped them together and called this potpourri Black Studies....

"A Black Feminist Statement" (1977)

The Combahee River Collective

Radical Black feminist writers and activists Barbara Smith, Demita Fra-
zier, and Beverly Smith together drafted the Combahee River Collective
statement in 1977. Widely considered to be one of the most influential
Black feminist documents of the twentieth century, the statement centers
the contributions and theorizations of queer Black feminists to the long
Black freedom movement while also underscoring the importance of orga-
nizing across difference.

Above all else, our politics initially sprang from the shared belief that black
women are inherently valuable, that our liberation is a necessity not as an ad-
junct to somebody else's but because of our need as human persons for autonomy. This may seem so obvious as to sound simplistic, but it is apparent that no
other ostensibly progressive movement has ever considered our specific oppression as a priority or worked seriously for the ending of that oppression. The mere
names of the pejorative stereotypes attributed to black women (e.g., mammy,
matriarch, Sapphire, whore, bulldagger), let alone cataloguing the cruel, often
murderous, treatment we receive, indicates how little value has been placed
upon our lives during four centuries of bondage in the Western hemisphere. We
realize that the only people who care enough about us to work consistently for
our liberation is us. Our politics evolve from a healthy love for ourselves, our
sisters, and our community, which allows us to continue our struggle and work.

This focusing upon our own oppression is embodied in the concept of identity politics. We believe that the most profound and potentially the most radical

politics come directly out of our own identity, as opposed to working to end somebody else's oppression. In the case of black women this is a particularly repugnant, dangerous, threatening, and therefore revolutionary concept because it is obvious from looking at all the political movements that have preceded us that anyone is more worthy of liberation than ourselves. We reject pedestals, queenhood, and walking ten paces behind. To be recognized as human, levelly human, is enough.

We believe that sexual politics under patriarchy is as pervasive in black women's lives as are the politics of class and race. We also often find it difficult to separate race from class from sex oppression because in our lives they are most often experienced simultaneously. We know that there is such a thing as racial-sexual oppression that is neither solely racial nor solely sexual, e.g., the history of rape of black women by white men as a weapon of political repression.

Although we are feminists and lesbians, we feel solidarity with progressive black men and do not advocate the fractionalization that white women who are separatists demand. Our situation as black people necessitates that we have solidarity around the fact of race, which white women of course do not need to have with white men, unless it is their negative solidarity as racial oppressors. We struggle together with black men against racism, while we also struggle with black men about sexism.

We realize that the liberation of all oppressed peoples necessitates the destruction of the political-economic systems of capitalism and imperialism as well as patriarchy. We are socialists because we believe the work must be organized for the collective benefit of those who do the work and create the products and not for the profit of the bosses. Material resources must be equally distributed among those who create these resources. We are not convinced, however, that a socialist revolution that is not also a feminist and antiracist revolution will guarantee our liberation. We have arrived at the necessity for developing an understanding of class relationships that takes into account the specific class position of black women who are generally marginal in the labor force, while at this particular time some of us are temporarily viewed as doubly desirable tokens at white-collar and professional levels. We need to articulate the real class situation of persons who are not merely raceless, sexless workers, but for whom racial and sexual oppression are significant determinants in their working/economic lives. Although we are in essential agreement with Marx's theory as it applied to the very specific economic relationships he analyzed, we know that this analysis must be extended further in order for us to understand our specific economic situation as black women.

"Toward a Black Feminist Criticism" (1977)

Barbara Smith

Barbara Smith is cofounder of the Combahee River Collective and one of the authors of the influential Combahee River Collective statement (1977). Her work is situated at the intersection of Black feminism and Black queer studies. In 1980, she cofounded Kitchen Table: Women of Color Press, the first US-based publisher of books for women of color. In "Toward a Black Feminist Criticism," excerpted below, Smith argues for the importance of creating space and platforms "for the exploration of black women's lives and the creation of consciously black women-identified art."

Long before I tried to write this I felt that I was attempting something un-precedented, something dangerous merely by writing about Black women writers from a feminist perspective and about Black lesbian writers from any perspective at all. These things have not been done. Not by white male critics, expectedly. Not by Black male critics. Not by white women critics who think of themselves as feminists. And most crucially not by Black women critics who, although they pay the most attention to Black women writers as a group, sel-dom use a consistent feminist analysis or write about Black lesbian literature. All segments of the literary world—whether establishment, progressive, Black, female, or lesbian—do not know, or at least act as if they do not know, that Black women writers and Black lesbian writers exist.

For whites, this specialized lack of knowledge is inextricably connected to their not knowing in any concrete or politically transforming way that Black women of any description dwell in this place. Black women's existence, experience, and culture, and the brutally complex systems of oppression which shape these, are in the "real world" of white and/or male consciousness beneath consideration, invisible, unknown.

This invisibility, which goes beyond anything that either Black men or white women experience and tell about in their writing, is one reason it is so difficult for me to know where to start. It seems overwhelming to break such a massive silence. Even more numbing, however, is the realization that so many of the women who will read this have not yet noticed us missing either from their reading matter, their politics, or their lives. It is galling that ostensible feminists and acknowledged lesbians have been so blinded to the implications of any womanhood that is not white womanhood and that they have yet to struggle with the deep racism in themselves that is at the source of this blindness.

I think of the thousands and thousands of books, magazines, and articles which have been devoted, by this time, to the subject of women's writing and I am filled with rage at the fraction of those pages that mention Black and other Third-World women. I finally do not know how to begin because in 1978 I want to be writing this for a Black feminist publication, for Black women who know and love these writers as I do and who, if they do not yet know their names, have at least profoundly felt the pain of their absence.

The conditions that coalesce into the impossibilities of this essay have as much to do with politics as with the practice of literature. Any discussion of Afro-American writers can rightfully begin with the fact that for most of the time we have been in this country we have been categorically denied not only literacy, but the most minimal possibility of a decent human life. In her landmark essay, "In Search of Our Mothers' Gardens," Alice Walker discloses how the political, economic and social restrictions of slavery and racism have historically stunted the creative lives of Black women.

At the present time I feel that the politics of feminism have a direct relationship to the state of Black women's literature. A viable, autonomous Black feminist movement in this country would open up the space needed for the exploration of Black women's lives and the creation of consciously Black woman-identified art. At the same time a redefinition of the goals and strategies of the white feminist movement would lead to much needed change in the focus and content of what is now generally accepted as women's culture.

"The Lost Races of Science Fiction" (1980)

Octavia Butler

Perhaps best known as a writer of science fiction, Octavia Butler's (1947–2006) work challenges the Eurocentrism of the genre. Through her trenchant examinations of racial injustice, women's rights, the climate crisis, and beyond, Butler's writing helped to support the emerging subgenre of Afrofuturism. In her 1980 essay "The Lost Races of Science Fiction"— excerpted below—Butler explores why "Blacks, Asians, Hispanics, Amerindians, [and] minority characters in general have been noticeably absent from most science fiction" and critiques the genre's unwillingness to "reach into the lives of ordinary everyday humans who happen not to be white."

Fourteen years ago, during my first year of college, I sat in a creative writing class and listened as my teacher, an elderly man, told another student not to use black characters in his stories unless those characters' blackness was somehow essential to the plots. The presence of blacks, my teacher felt, changed the focus of a story, drew attention from the intended subject.

This happened in 1965. I would never have expected to hear my teacher's sentiments echoed by a science fiction writer in 1979. Hear them I did, though, at a science fiction convention where a writer explained that he had decided against using a black character in one of his stories because the presence of the black would change his story somehow. Later, this same writer suggested that in stories that seem to require black characters to make some racial point, it might be possible to substitute extraterrestrials—so as not to dwell on matters of race.

Well, let's do a little dwelling.

Science fiction reaches into the future, the past, the human mind. It reaches out to other worlds and into other dimensions. Is it really so limited, then, that it cannot reach into the lives of ordinary everyday humans who happen not to be white?

Blacks, Asians, Hispanics, Amerindians, minority characters in general have been noticeably absent from most science fiction. Why? As a black and a science fiction writer, I've heard that question often. I've also heard several answers. And, because most people try to be polite, there have been certain answers I haven't heard. That's all right. They're obvious.

Best, though, and most hopeful from my point of view, I've heard from people who want to write science fiction, or who've written a few pieces, perhaps, and who would like to include minority characters, but aren't sure how to go about it. Since I've had to solve the same problem in reverse, maybe I can help.

But first some answers to my question: Why have there been so few minority characters in science fiction?

Let's examine my teacher's reason. Are minority characters—black characters in this case—so disruptive a force that the mere presence of one alters a story, focuses it on race rather than whatever the author had in mind? Yes, in fact, black characters can do exactly that if the creators of those characters are too restricted in their thinking to visualize blacks in any other context.

This is the kind of stereotyping, conscious or subconscious, that women have fought for so long. No writer who regards blacks as people, human beings, with the usual variety of human concerns, flaws, skills, hopes, etc., would have trouble creating interesting backgrounds and goals for black characters. No writer who regards blacks as people would get sidetracked into justifying their blackness or their presence unless such justification honestly played a part in the story. It is no more necessary to focus on a character's blackness than it is to focus on a woman's femininity.

Now, what about the possibility of substituting extra-terrestrials for blacks—in order to make some race-related point without making anyone . . . uncomfortable? In fact, why can't blacks be represented by whites—who are not too thoroughly described—thus leaving readers free to use their imaginations and visualize whichever color they like?

I usually manage to go on being polite when I hear questions like these, but it's not easy. . . .

And as for whites representing all of humanity—on the theory that people will imagine other races; or better yet, on the theory that all people are alike anyway, so what does it matter? Well, remember when men represented all of humanity? Women didn't care much for it. Still don't. No great mental leap is required to understand why blacks, why any minority, might not care much for it either. And apart from all that, of course, it doesn't work. Whites represent themselves, and that's plenty. Spread the burden.

Back when *Star Wars* was new, a familiar excuse for ignoring minorities went something like this: "Science fiction is escapist literature. Its readers/viewers don't want to be weighted down with real problems." War, okay. Planet-wide destruction, okay. Kidnapping, okay. But the sight of a minority person? Too heavy. Too real....

"Foreword, 1981" from
This Bridge Called My Back:
Writings by Radical Women of Color (1981)

Toni Cade Bambara

An accomplished and prolific writer, thinker, filmmaker, and scholar,
Toni Cade Bambara (1939–1995) used her voice to uplift, amplify, and
be in solidarity with other women of color working toward collective
freedom. Perhaps best known for her short essays and novels, Bamba-
ra's writing played with the hard-and-fast notion of genre. Excerpted
below, Bambara's foreword to This Bridge Called My Back: Writings
by Radical Women of Color *(edited by Cherríe Moraga and Gloria*
Anzaldúa) argues for the power of building women of color–led political
alliances in the fight against the conjoined violence of patriarchy and
white supremacy.

Now that we've begun to break the silence and begun to break through the dia-
bolically erected barriers and can hear each other and see each other, we can sit
down with trust and break bread together. Rise up and break our chains as well.
For though the initial motive of several siter/riters here may have been to protest, complain or explain to white feminist would-be allies that there are other
ties and visions that bind, prior allegiances and priorities that supercede their
invitations to coalesce on their terms ("Assimilation within a solely western-
european herstory is not acceptable" —Lorde), the process of examining that

would-be alliance awakens us to new tasks ("We have a lot more to concentrate on beside the pathology of white wimmin." —davenport)

and a new connection:	US
a new set of recognitions:	US
a new site of accountability:	US
a new set of power:	US

And the possibilities intuited here or alluded to there or called forth in various pieces in flat out talking in tongues—the possibility of several million women refuting the numbers game inherent in "minority," the possibility of denouncing the insulated/orchestrated conflict game of divide and conquer—through the fashioning of potent networks of all the daughters of the ancient mother cultures is awesome, mighty, a glorious life work. *This Bridge* lays down the planks to cross over on to a new place where stooped labor cramped quartered down pressed and caged up combatants can straighten the spine and expand the lungs and make the vision manifest ("The dream is real, my friends. The failure to realize it is the only unreality." —Street Preacher in *The Salt Eaters*).

This Bridge documents particular rites of passage. Coming of age and coming to terms with community—race, group, class, gender, self perversions—racism, prejudice, elitism, misogyny, homophobia, and murder. And coming to terms with the incorporation of disease, struggling to overthrow the internal colonial, pro-racist loyalties—color/hue/hair caste within the household, power perversities engaged in under the guise of "personal relationships," accommodation to and collaboration with self-ambush and amnesia and murder. And coming to grips with those false awakenings too that give us ease as we substitute a militant mouth for a radical politic, delaying our true coming of age as committed, competent, principled combatants....

. . . We have got to know each other better and teach each other our ways, our views, if we are to remove the scales ("seeing radical differences where they don't exist and not seeing them where they are critical" —Quintanales) and get the work done.

This Bridge can get us there. Can coax us into the habit of listening to each other and learning each other's ways of seeing and being. Of hearing each other as we heard each other in Pat Lee's Freshtones, as we heard each other in Pat

Jones and Faye Chiang, et al.'s Ordinary Women, as we heard each other in Fran Beale's Third World Women's Alliance newspaper. As we heard each other over the years in snatched time moments in hallways and conference corridors, caucusing between sets. As we heard each other in those split second interfacings of yours and mine and hers student union meetings. As we heard each other in that rainbow attempt under the auspices of IFCO years ago. And way before that when Chinese, Mexican, and African women in this country saluted each other's attempts to form protective leagues. And before that when New Orleans African women and Yamassee and Yamacrow women went into the swamps to meet with Filipino wives of "draftees" and "defectors" during the so-called French and Indian War. And when members of the maroon communities and women of the long lodge held council together while the Seminole Wars raged. And way way before that, before the breaking of the land mass when we mothers of the yam, of the rice, of the maize, of the plantain sat together in a circle, staring into the camp fire, the answers in our laps, knowing how to focus....

Quite frankly, *This Bridge* needs no Foreword. It is the Afterword that'll count. The coalitions of women determined to be a danger to our enemies, as June Jordan would put it. The will to be dangerous ("ask billie so we can learn how to have those bigtime bigdaddies jumping outta windows and otherwise offing theyselves in droves" —gossett). And the contracts we creative combatants will make to mutually care and cure each other into wholesomeness. And blue-prints we will draw up of the new order we will make manifest. And the personal unction we will discover in the mirror, in the dreams, or on the path across *This Bridge*. The work: To make revolution irresistible.

"Introduction: The Politics of Black Women's Studies" from *All the Women Are White, All the Blacks Are Men, But Some of Us Are Brave: Black Women's Studies* (1982)

Gloria T. Hull and Barbara Smith

Written by Black feminist poet, educator, and social critic Gloria T. Hull and Barbara Smith (see fuller bio on "Toward a Black Feminist Criticism," page 78), "Introduction: The Politics of Black Women's Studies" from All the Women Are White, All the Blacks Are Men, But Some of Us Are Brave: Black Women's Studies *helps to map the politics of Black women's studies and describes its origins, content, and objectives. Excerpted below, their introduction calls unflinchingly for "Black women to carry out autonomously defined investigations of self in a society which through racial, sexual, and class oppression systematically denies our existence."*

Merely to use the term "Black women's studies" is an act charged with political significance. At the very least, the combining of these words to name a discipline means taking the stance that Black women exist—and exist positively—a stance that is in direct opposition to most of what passes for culture and thought on the North American continent. To use the term and to act on it in a white-male world is an act of political courage.

Like any politically diseenfranchised group, Black women could not exist consciously until we began to name ourselves. The growth of Black women's studies is an essential aspect of that process of naming. The very fact that Black women's studies describes something that is really happening, a burgeoning field of study, indicates that there are political changes afoot which have made possible that growth. To examine the politics of Black women's studies means to consider not only what it is, but why it is and what it can be. Politics is used here in its widest sense to mean any situation/relationship of differential power between groups or individuals.

Four issues seem important for a consideration of the politics of Black women's studies: (1) the general political situation of Afro-American women and the bearing this has had upon the implementation of Black women's studies; (2) the relationship of Black women's studies to Black feminist politics and the Black feminist movement; (3) the necessity for Black women's studies to be feminist, radical, and analytical; and (4) the need for teachers of Black women's studies to be aware of our problematic political positions in the academy and of the potentially antagonistic conditions under which we must work.

The political position of Black women in America has been, in a single word, embattled. The extremity of our oppression has been determined by our very biological identity. The horrors we have faced historically and continue to face as Black women in a white-male-dominated society have implications for every aspect of our lives, including what white men have termed "the life of the mind." That our oppression as Black women can take forms specifically aimed at discrediting our intellectual power is best illustrated through the words of a "classic" American writer.

In 1932 William Faulkner saw fit to include this sentence in a description of a painted sign in his novel *Light in August*. He wrote:

> But now and then a negro nursemaid with her white charges would loiter there and spell them [the letters on the sign] aloud with *that vacuous idiocy of her idle and illiterate kind.* [Italics ours]

Faulkner's white-male assessment of Black female intellect and character, stated as a mere aside, has fundamental and painful implications for a consideration of the whole question of Black women's studies and the politics that shape its existence. Not only does his remark typify the extremely negative ways in which Afro-American women have been portrayed in literature, scholarship, and the popular media, but it also points to the destructive white-male habit of categorizing all who are not like themselves as their intellectual and moral inferiors. The fact that the works in which such oppressive images appear are nevertheless considered American "masterpieces" indicates the cultural-political value system in which Afro-American women have been forced to operate and which, when possible, they have actively opposed.

The politics of Black women's studies are totally connected to the politics of Black women's lives in this country. The opportunities for Black women to carry out autonomously defined investigations of self in a society which through racial, sexual, and class oppression systematically denies our existence have been by definition limited.

As a major result of the historical realities which brought us enslaved to this continent, we have been kept separated in every way possible from recognized intellectual work. Our legacy as chattel, as sexual slaves as well as forced laborers, would adequately explain why most Black women are, to this day, far away from the centers of academic power and why Black women's studies has just begun to surface in the latter part of the 1970s. What our multilayered oppression does not explain are the ways in which we have created and maintained our own intellectual traditions as Black women, without either the recognition or the support of white-male society. . . .

The inception of Black women's studies can be directly traced to three significant political movements of the twentieth century. These are the struggles for Black liberation and women's liberation, which themselves fostered the growth of Black and women's studies, and the more recent Black feminist movement, which is just beginning to show its strength. Black feminism has made a space for Black women's studies to exist and, through its commitment to all Black women, will provide the basis for its survival.

The history of all of these movements is unique, yet interconnected. The Black movements of the 1950s, '60s, and '70s brought about unprecedented social and political change, not only in the lives of Black people, but for all Americans. The early women's movement gained inspiration from the Black movement as well as an impetus to organize autonomously both as a result of the demands for all-Black organizations and in response to sexual hierarchies in Black- and white-male political groupings. Black women were a part of that early women's movement, as were working-class women of all races. However, for many reasons—including the increasing involvement of single, middle-class white women (who often had the most time to devote to political work), the divisive campaigns of the white-male media, and the movement's serious inability to deal with racism—the women's movement became largely and apparently white.

The effect that this had upon the nascent field of women's studies was predictably disastrous. Women's studies courses, usually taught in universities, which could be considered elite institutions just by virtue of the populations they served, focused almost exclusively upon the lives of white women. Black studies, which was much too often male-dominated, also ignored Black women....

Because of white women's racism and Black men's sexism, there was no room in either area for a serious consideration of the lives of Black women. And even when they have considered Black women, white women usually have not had the capacity to analyze racial politics and Black culture, and Black men have remained blind or resistant to the implications of sexual politics in Black women's lives.

Only a Black *and* feminist analysis can sufficiently comprehend the materials of Black women's studies; and only a creative Black feminist perspective will enable the field to expand. A viable Black feminist movement will also lend its political strength to the development of Black women's studies courses, programs, and research, and to the funding they require. Black feminism's total commitment to the liberation of Black women and its recognition of Black women as valuable and complex human beings will provide the analysis and spirit for the most incisive work on Black women. Only a feminist, pro-woman perspective that acknowledges the reality of sexual oppression in the lives of Black women, as well as the oppression of race and class, will make Black women's studies the transformer of consciousness it needs to be.

Women's studies began as a radical response to feminists' realization that knowledge of ourselves has been deliberately kept from us by institutions of patriarchal "learning." Unfortunately, as women's studies has become both more institutionalized and at the same time more precarious within traditional academic structures, the radical life-changing vision of what women's studies can accomplish has constantly been diminished in exchange for acceptance, respectability, and the career advancement of individuals. This trend in women's studies is a trap that Black women's studies cannot afford to fall into. Because we are

so oppressed as Black women, every aspect of our fight for freedom, including
teaching and writing about ourselves, must in some way further our liberation.
Because of the particular history of Black feminism in relation to Black women's
studies, especially the fact that the two movements are still new and have evolved
nearly simultaneously, much of the current teaching, research, and writing about
Black women is not feminist, is not radical, and unfortunately is not always even
analytical. Naming and describing our experience are important initial steps,
but not alone sufficient to get us where we need to go. A descriptive approach to
the lives of Black women, a "great Black women" in history or literature approach,
or any traditional male-identified approach, will not result in intellectually
groundbreaking or politically transforming work. We cannot change our lives
by teaching solely about "exceptions" to the ravages of white-male oppression.
Only through exploring the experience of supposedly "ordinary" Black women
whose "unexceptional" actions enabled us and the race to survive, will we be able
to begin to develop an overview and an analytical framework for understanding
the lives of Afro-American women. . . .

   An accountable Black women's studies would value all Black women's experiences. Yet for a Black woman to teach a course on Black lesbians would probably, in most universities, spell career suicide, not to mention the personal and
emotional repercussions she would inevitably face. Even to teach Black women's
studies from a principled Black feminist perspective might endanger many Black
women scholars' situations in their schools and departments. Given the difficulty
and risks involved in teaching information and ideas which the white-male academy does not recognize or approve, it is important for Black women teaching in
the white-male academy always to realize the inherently contradictory and antagonistic nature of the conditions under which we do our work. These working
conditions exist in a structure not only elitist and racist, but deeply misogynist.
Often our position as Black women is dishearteningly tenuous within university walls: we are literally the last hired and the first fired. Despite popular myths
about the advantages of being "double-tokens," our salaries, promotions, tenure,
and general level of acceptance in the white-male "community of scholars" are all
quite grim. The current backlash against affirmative action is also disastrous for
all Black women workers, including college teachers.

   As Black women we belong to two groups that have been defined as con-
genitally inferior in intellect, that is, Black people and women. The paradox of

Black women's position is well illustrated by the fact that white-male academics, like Schockley and Jensen—in the very same academy—are trying to prove "scientifically" our racial and sexual inferiority. Their overt or tacit question is, "How could a being, who combines two mentally deficient biological identities, do anything with her intellect, her nonexistent powers of mind?" Or, to put it more bluntly, "How can someone who looks like my maid (or my fantasy of my maid) teach me anything?" ...

To do the work involved in creating Black women's studies requires not only intellectual intensity, but the deepest courage. Ideally, this is passionate and committed research, writing, and teaching whose purpose is to question everything. Coldly "objective" scholarship that changes nothing is not what we strive for. "Objectivity" is itself an example of the reification of white-male thought. What could be less objective than the totally white-male studies which are still considered "knowledge"? Everything that human beings participate in is ultimately subjective and biased, and there is nothing inherently wrong with that. The bias of Black women's studies must consider as primary the knowledge that will save Black women's lives.

"Black Women: Shaping Feminist Theory" from *Feminist Theory: From Margin to Center*

(1984)

bell hooks

bell hooks (1952–2021) was a prolific and influential Black feminist poet, writer, cultural critic, and scholar whose work centered the lives of Black women and critiqued the mainstream feminist movement's reflex to privilege the experiences of white women. Located at the intersection of race, gender, sexuality, and place, hooks's scholarship often highlighted the connections among love, organizing, and freedom. Excerpted below, hooks's writing in her magisterial Feminist Theory: From Margin to Center *(1984) calls for Black women to recognize "the special vantage point our marginality gives us and make use of this perspective to criticize the dominant racist, classist, sexist hegemony as well as to envision and create a counter-hegemony."*

. . . My awareness of feminist struggle was stimulated by social circumstance. Growing up in a Southern, black, father-dominated, working-class household, I experienced (as did my mother, my sisters, and my brother) varying degrees of patriarchal tyranny and it made me angry—it made us all angry. Anger led me to question the politics of male dominance and enabled me to resist sexist socialization. Frequently, white feminists act as if black women did not know sexist oppression existed until they voiced feminist sentiment. They believe they are providing black women with "the" analysis and "the" program for liberation. They do not understand, cannot even imagine, that black women, as well as other groups of women who live daily in oppressive situations, often acquire an awareness of patriarchal politics from their lived experience, just as they develop strategies of resistance (even though they may not resist on a sustained or organized basis).

These black women observed white feminist focus on male tyranny and women's oppression as if it were a "new" revelation, and felt such a focus had little impact on their lives. To them it was just another indication of the privileged living conditions of middle- and upper-class white women that they would need a theory to inform them that they were "oppressed." The implication being that people who are truly oppressed know it even though they may not be engaged in organized resistance or are unable to articulate in written form the nature of their oppression. These black women saw nothing liberatory in party-line analyses of women's oppression. Neither the fact that black women have not organized collectively in huge numbers around the issues of "feminism" (many of us do not know or use the term) nor the fact that we have not had access to the machinery of power that would allow us to share our analyses or theories about gender with the American public negate its presence in our lives or places us in a position of dependency in relationship to those white and non white feminists who address a larger audience.

The understanding I had by age thirteen of patriarchal politics created in me expectations of the feminist movement that were quite different from those of young, middle-class, white women. When I entered my first women's studies class at Stanford University in the early 1970s, white women were reveling in the joy of being together—to them it was an important, momentous occasion. I had not known a life where women had not been together, where women had not helped, protected, and loved one another deeply. I had not known white women who were ignorant of the impact of race and class on their social status and consciousness. (Southern white women often have a more realistic perspective on racism and classism than white women in other areas of the United States.) I did not feel sympathetic to white peers who maintained that I could not expect them to have knowledge of or understand the life experiences of black women. Despite my background (living in racially segregated communities) I knew about the lives of white women, and certainly no white women lived in our neighborhood, attended our schools, or worked in our homes.

When I participated in feminist groups, I found that white women adopted a condescending attitude towards me and other non-white participants. The condescension they directed at black women was one of the means they employed to remind us that the women's movement was "theirs"—that we were able to participate because they allowed it, even encouraged it; after all, we were needed to legitimate the process. They did not see us as equals. They did not treat us as equals. And though they expected us to provide first-hand accounts of black experience, they felt it was their role to decide if these experiences were authentic. Frequently, college-educated black women (even those from poor and working-class backgrounds) were dismissed as mere imitators. Our presence in movement activities did not count, as white women were convinced that "real" blackness meant speaking the patois of poor black people, being uneducated, streetwise, and a variety of other stereotypes. If we dared to criticize the movement or to assume responsibility for reshaping feminist ideas and introducing new ideas, our voices were tuned out, dismissed, silenced. We could be heard only if our statements echoed the sentiments of the dominant discourse.

Attempts by white feminists to silence black women are rarely written about. All too often they have taken place in conference rooms, classrooms, or the privacy of cozy living-room settings, where one lone black woman faces the racist hostility of a group of white women. From the time the women's liberation movement began, individual black women went to groups. Many never returned after a first meeting. Anita Cornwall is correct in "Three for the Price of One: Notes from a Gay Black Feminist," when she states, "Sadly enough, fear of encountering racism seems to be one of the main reasons that so many black women refuse to join the women's movement." Recent focus on the issue of racism has generated discourse but has had little impact on the behavior of white feminists towards black women. Often the white women who are busy publishing papers and books on "unlearning racism" remain patronizing and condescending when they relate to black women. This is not surprising given that frequently their discourse is aimed solely in the direction of a white audience and the focus solely on changing attitudes rather than addressing racism in a historical and political context. They make us the "objects" of their privileged discourse on race. As "objects," we remain unequals, inferiors. Even though they may be sincerely concerned about racism, their methodology suggests they are not yet free of the type of paternalism endemic to white supremacist ideology. Some of these women place themselves in the position of "authorities" who must mediate communication between racist white women (naturally they see themselves as having come to terms with their racism) and angry black women whom they believe are incapable of rational discourse. Of course, the system of racism, classism, and educational elitism must remain intact if they are to maintain their authoritative positions....

...White women and black men have it both ways. They can act as oppressor or be oppressed. Black men may be victimized by racism, but sexism allows them to act as exploiters and oppressors of women. White women may be victimized by sexism, but racism enables them to act as exploiters and oppressors of black people. Both groups have led liberation movements that favor their interests and support the continued oppression of other groups. Black male sexism has undermined struggles to eradicate racism just as white female racism undermines feminist struggle. As long as these two groups, or any group, defines liberation as gaining social equality with ruling-class white men, they have a vested interest in the continued exploitation and oppression of others.

Black women with no institutionalized "other" that we may discriminate against, exploit, or oppress often have a lived experience that directly challenges the prevailing classist, sexist, racist social structure and its concomitant ideology. This lived experience may shape our consciousness in such a way that our world view differs from those who have a degree of privilege (however relative within the existing system). It is essential for continued feminist struggle that black women recognize the special vantage point our marginality gives us and make use of this perspective to criticize the dominant racist, classist, sexist hegemony as well as to envision and create a counter-hegemony. I am suggesting that we have a central role to play in the making of feminist theory and a contribution to offer that is unique and valuable. The formation of a liberatory feminist theory and praxis is a collective responsibility, one that must be shared. Though I criticize aspects of feminist movement as we have known it so far, a critique which is sometimes harsh and unrelenting, I do so not in an attempt to diminish feminist struggle but to enrich, to share in the work of making a liberatory ideology and a liberatory movement.

"The Race for Theory" (1987)

Barbara Christian

Barbara Christian (1943–2000) is widely recognized as a leading scholar in Black literary criticism. She is perhaps best known for Black Women Novelists: The Development of a Tradition *(1980) and the essay "The Race for Theory," which is excerpted below. She famously asks, "For whom are we doing what we are doing when we do literary criticism?" Writing against theory as a mere intellectual exercise, Christian memorably notes: "What I write and how I write is done in order to save my own life. And I mean that literally. For me, literature is a way of knowing that I am not hallucinating, that whatever I feel/know is."*

I have seized this occasion to break the silence among those of us, critics, as we are now called, who have been intimidated, devalued by what I call the race for theory. I have become convinced that there has been a takeover in the literary world by Western philosophers from the old literary elite, the neutral humanists. Philosophers have been able to effect such a takeover because so much of the literature of the West has become pallid, laden with despair, self-indulgent, and disconnected. The New Philosophers, eager to understand a world that is today fast escaping political control, have redefined literature so that the distinctions implied by that term, that is, the distinctions between everything written and those things written to evoke feeling as well as to express thought, have been blurred. They have changed literary critical language to suit their own purposes as philosophers, and they have reinvented the meaning of theory.

My first response to this realization was to ignore it. Perhaps, in spite of the egocentrism of this trend, some good might come of it. I had, I felt, more pressing and interesting things to do, such as reading and studying the history and literature of black women, a history that had been totally ignored, a contemporary literature bursting with originality, passion, insight, and beauty. But, unfortunately, it is difficult to ignore this new takeover, because theory has become a commodity that helps determine whether we are hired or promoted in academic institutions—worse, whether we are heard at all. Due to this new orientation, works (a word that evokes labor) have become texts. Critics are no longer concerned with literature but with other critics' texts, for the critic yearning for attention has displaced the writer and has conceived of herself or himself as the center. Interestingly, in the first part of this century, at least in England and America, the critic was usually also a writer of poetry, plays, or novels. But today, as a new generation of professionals develops, she or he is increasingly an academic. Activities such as teaching or writing one's response to specific works of literature have, among this group, become subordinated to one primary thrust—that moment when one creates a theory, thus fixing a constellation of ideas for a time at least, a fixing which no doubt will be replaced in another month or so by somebody else's competing theory as the race accelerates. Perhaps because those who have effected the takeover have the power (although they deny it) first of all to be published, and thereby to determine the ideas that are deemed valuable, some of our most daring and potentially radical critics (and by *our* I mean black, women, Third World) have been influenced, even co-opted, into speaking a language and defining their discussion in terms alien to and opposed to our needs and orientation. At least so far, the creative writers I study have resisted this language.

For people of color have always theorized—but in forms quite different from the Western form of abstract logic. And I am inclined to say that our theorizing (and I intentionally use the verb rather than the noun) is often in narrative forms, in the stories we create, in riddles and proverbs, in the play with language, because dynamic rather than fixed ideas seem more to our liking. How else have we managed to survive with such spiritedness the assault on our bodies, social institutions, countries, our very humanity? And women, at least the women I grew up around, continuously speculated about the nature of life through pithy language that unmasked the power relations of their world. It is this language, and the grace and pleasure with which they played with it, that I find celebrated, refined, critiqued in the works of writers like Toni Morrison and Alice Walker. My folk, in other words, have always been a race for theory—though more in the form of the hieroglyph, a written figure that is both sensual and abstract, both beautiful and communicative. In my own work I try to illuminate and explain these hieroglyphs, which is, I think, an activity quite different from the creating of the hieroglyphs themselves. As the Buddhists would say, the finger pointing at the moon is not the moon.

In this discussion, however, I am more concerned with the issue raised by my first use of the term, *the race for theory*, in relation to its academic hegemony, and possibly of its inappropriateness to the energetic emerging literatures in the world today. The pervasiveness of this academic hegemony is an issue continually spoken about—but usually in hidden groups, lest we, who are disturbed by it, appear ignorant to the reigning academic elite. Among the folk who speak in muted tones are people of color, feminists, radical critics, creative writers, who have struggled for much longer than a decade to make their voices, their various voices, heard, and for whom literature is not an occasion for discourse among critics but is necessary nourishment for their people and one way by which they come to understand their lives better. Clichéd though this may be, it bears, I think, repeating here.

The race for theory—with its linguistic jargon; its emphasis on quoting its prophets; its tendency toward "biblical" exegesis; its refusal even to mention specific works of creative writers, far less contemporary ones; its preoccupations with mechanical analyses of language, graphs, algebraic equations; its gross generalizations about culture—has silenced many of us to the extent that some of us feel we can no longer discuss our own literature, and others have developed intense writing blocks and are puzzled by the incomprehensibility of the language set adrift in literary circles. There have been, in the last year, any number of occasions on which I had to convince literary critics who have pioneered entire new areas of critical inquiry that they did have something to say. Some of us are continually harassed to invent wholesale theories regardless of the complexity of the literature we study. I, for one, am tired of being asked to produce a black feminist literary theory as if I were a mechanical man. For I believe such theory is prescriptive—it ought to have some relationship to practice. Because I can count on one hand the number of people attempting to be black feminist literary critics in the world today, I consider it presumptuous of me to invent a theory of how we *ought* to read. Instead, I think we need to read the works of our writers in our various ways and remain open to the intricacies of the intersection of language, class, race, and gender in the literature. And it would help if we share our process, that is, our practice, as much as possible because, finally, our work *is* a collective endeavor.

The insidious quality of this race for theory is symbolized for me by a term like "minority discourse," a label that is borrowed from the reigning theory of the day but which is untrue to the literatures being produced by our writers, for many of our literatures (certainly Afro-American literature) are central, not minor. I have used the passive voice in my last sentence construction, contrary to the rules of black English, which like all languages has a particular value system, because I have not placed reponsibility on any particular person or group. But that is precisely because this new ideology has become so prevalent among us that it behaves like so many of the other ideologies with which we have had to contend. It appears to have neither head nor center. At the least, though, we can say that the terms "minority" and "discourse" are located firmly in a Western dualistic or "binary" frame which sees the rest of the world as minor and tries to convince the rest of the world that it *is* major, usually through force and then through language, even as it claims many of the ideas that we, its "historical" other, have known and spoken about for so long. For many of us have never conceived of ourselves only as somebody's *other*. . . .

My major objection to the race for theory, as some readers have probably guessed by now, really hinges on the question, "For whom are we doing what we are doing when we do literary criticism?" It is, I think, the central question today, especially for the few of us who have infiltrated the academy enough to be wooed by it. The answer to that question determines what orientation we take in our work, the language we use, the purposes for which it is intended.

I can only speak for myself. But what I write and how I write is done in order to save my own life. And I mean that literally. For me, literature is a way of knowing that I am not hallucinating, that whatever I feel/know *is*. . . .

"The Social Construction of Black Feminist Thought" (1989)

Patricia Hill Collins

Focusing on the intersection of race, gender, class, nation, and knowledge production, Patricia Hill Collins is a leading figure in Black feminist thought. Writing on the relationship between politics and epistemology, Collins argues in "The Social Construction of Black Feminist Thought"—excerpted below—that Black women's experience can serve as a ground for creating ways of knowing that "calls into question the content of what currently passes as truth and simultaneously challenges the process of arriving at that truth."

Living life as an African-American woman is a necessary prerequisite for producing Black feminist thought because within Black women's communities thought is validated and produced with reference to a particular set of historical, material, and epistemological conditions. African-American women who adhere to the idea that claims about Black women must be substantiated by Black women's sense of their own experiences and who anchor their knowledge claims in an Afrocentric feminist epistemology have produced a rich tradition of Black feminist thought.

Traditionally, such women were blues singers, poets, autobiographers, storytellers, and orators validated by the larger community of Black women as experts on a Black women's standpoint. Only a few unusual African-American feminist scholars have been able to defy Eurocentric masculinist epistemologies and explicitly embrace an Afrocentric feminist epistemology. Consider Alice Walker's description of Zora Neale Hurston: "In my mind, Zora Neale Hurston, Billie Holiday, and Bessie Smith form a sort of unholy trinity. Zora *belongs* in the tradition of Black women singers, rather than among 'the literati.' . . . Like Billie and Bessie she followed her own road, believed in her own gods, pursued her own dreams, and refused to separate herself from 'common' people."

Zora Neale Hurston is an exception for, prior to 1950, few Black women earned advanced degrees, and most of those who did complied with Euro-centric masculinist epistemologies. While these women worked on behalf of Black women, they did so within the confines of pervasive race and gender op-pression. Black women scholars were in a position to see the exclusion of Black women from scholarly discourse, and the thematic content of their work often reflected their interest in examining a Black women's standpoint. However, their tenuous status in academic institutions led them to adhere to Eurocentric masculinist epistemologies so that their work would be accepted as scholarly. As a result, while they produced Black feminist thought, those Black women most likely to gain academic credentials were often least likely to produce Black feminist thought that used an Afrocentric feminist epistemology.

As more Black women earn advanced degrees, the range of Black feminist scholarship is expanding. Increasing numbers of African-American women scholars are explicitly choosing to ground their work in Black women's expe-riences, and, by doing so, many implicitly adhere to an Afrocentric feminist epistemology. Rather than being restrained by their "both/and" status of mar-ginality, these women make creative use of their outsider-within status and produce innovative Black feminist thought. The difficulties these women face lie less in demonstrating the technical components of white male epistemolo-gies than in resisting the hegemonic nature of these patterns of thought in order to see, value, and use existing alternative Afrocentric feminist ways of knowing.

In establishing the legitimacy of their knowledge claims, Black women scholars who want to develop Black feminist thought may encounter the often conflicting standards of three key groups. First, Black feminist thought must be validated by ordinary African-American women who grow to woman-hood "in a world where the saner you are, the madder you are made to appear." To be credible in the eyes of this group, scholars must be personal advocates for their material, be accountable for the consequences of their work, have lived or experienced their material in some fashion, and be willing to engage in dialogues about their findings with ordinary, everyday people. Second, if it is to establish its legitimacy, Black feminist thought also must be accepted by the community of Black women scholars. These scholars place varying amounts of importance on rearticulating a Black women's standpoint using an Afrocentric feminist epistemology. Third, Black feminist thought within academia must be prepared to confront Eurocentric masculinist political and epistemological requirements.

The dilemma facing Black women scholars engaged in creating Black feminist thought is that a knowledge claim that meets the criteria of adequacy for one group and thus is judged to be an acceptable knowledge claim may not be translatable into the terms of a different group. Using the example of Black English, June Jordan illustrates the difficulty of moving among epistemologies: "You cannot 'translate' instances of Standard English preoccupied with abstraction or with nothing/nobody evidently alive into Black English. That would warp the language into uses antithetical to the guiding perspective of its community of users. Rather you must first change those Standard English sentences, themselves, into ideas consistent with the person-centered assumptions of Black English." While both worldviews share a common vocabulary, the ideas themselves defy direct translation.

Once Black feminist scholars face the notion that, on certain dimensions of a Black women's standpoint, it may be fruitless to try to translate ideas from an Afrocentric feminist epistemology into a Eurocentric masculinist epistemology, then the choices become clearer. Rather than trying to uncover universal knowledge claims that can withstand the translation from one epistemology to another, time might be better spent rearticulating a Black women's standpoint in order to give African-American women the tools to resist their own subordination. The goal here is not one of integrating Black female "folk culture" into the substantiated body of academic knowledge, for that substantiated knowledge is, in many ways, antithetical to the best interests of Black women. Rather, the process is one of rearticulating a preexisting Black women's standpoint and recentering the language of existing academic discourse to accommodate these knowledge claims. For those Black women scholars engaged in this rearticulation process, the social construction of Black feminist thought requires the skill and sophistication to decide which knowledge claims can be validated using the epistemological assumptions of one but not both frameworks, which claims can be generated in one framework and only partially accommodated by the other, and which claims can be made in both frameworks without violating the basic political and epistemological assumptions of either.

Black feminist scholars offering knowledge claims that cannot be accommodated by both frameworks face the choice between accepting the taken-for-granted assumptions that permeate white-male-controlled academic institutions or leaving academia. Those Black women who choose to remain in academia must accept the possibility that their knowledge claims will be limited to those claims about Black women that are consistent with a white male worldview. And yet those African-American women who leave academia may find their work is inaccessible to scholarly communities.

Black feminist scholars offering knowledge claims that can be partially accommodated by both epistemologies can create a body of thought that stands outside of either. Rather than trying to synthesize competing worldviews that, at this point in time, may defy reconciliation, their task is to point out common themes and concerns. By making creative use of their status as mediators, their thought becomes an entity unto itself that is rooted in two distinct political and epistemological contexts.

Those Black feminists who develop knowledge claims that both epistemologies can accommodate may have found a route to the elusive goal of generating so-called objective generalizations that can stand as universal truths. Those ideas that are validated as true by African-American women, African-American men, white men, white women, and other groups with distinctive standpoints, with each group using the epistemological approaches growing from its unique standpoint, thus become the most objective truths.

Alternative knowledge claims, in and of themselves, are rarely threatening to conventional knowledge. Such claims are routinely ignored, discredited, or simply absorbed and marginalized in existing paradigms. Much more threatening is the challenge that alternative epistemologies offer to the basic process used by the powerful to legitimate their knowledge claims. If the epistemology used to validate knowledge comes into question, then all prior knowledge claims validated under the dominant model become suspect. An alternative epistemology challenges all certified knowledge and opens up the question of whether what has been taken to be true can stand the test of alternative ways of validating truth. The existence of an independent Black women's standpoint using an Afrocentric feminist epistemology calls into question the content of what currently passes as truth and simultaneously challenges the process of arriving at that truth.

"African-American Women's History and the Metalanguage of Race" (1992)

Evelyn Brooks Higginbotham

Historian and scholar of race whose work ranges from the African American religious experience to Black women's history, Evelyn Brooks Higginbotham blends theory and history to tell the story of how Black people have worked to deconstruct "the dominant society's deployment of race." In the excerpt below from Higginbotham's "African-American Women's History and the Metalanguage of Race," she historicizes the very notion of race and explores the political uses to which it has been put.

As this culture of dissemblance illustrates, black people endeavored not only to silence and conceal but also to dismantle and deconstruct the dominant society's deployment of race. Racial meanings were never internalized by blacks and whites in an identical way. The language of race has historically been what Bakhtin calls a double-voiced discourse—serving the voice of black oppression and the voice of black liberation. Bakhtin observes: "The word in language is half someone else's. It becomes 'one's own' only when the speaker populates it with his [or her] own intention, his [or her] own accent, when he [or she] appropriates the word, adapting it to his [or her] own semantic and expressive intention." Blacks took "race" and empowered its language with their own meaning and intent, just as the slaves and freedpeople had appropriated white surnames, even those of their masters, and made their own.

For African-Americans, race signified a cultural identity that defined and connected them as a people, even as a nation. To be called a "race leader," "race man," or "race woman" by the black community was not a sign of insult or disapproval, nor did such titles refer to any and every black person. Quite to the contrary, they were conferred on Carter G. Woodson, W. E. B. Du Bois, Ida Wells-Barnett, Mary McLeod Bethune, and the other men and women who devoted their lives to the advancement of their people. When the National Association of Colored Women referred to its activities as "race work," it expressed both allegiance and commitment to the concerns of black people. Through a range of shifting, even contradictory meanings and accentuations expressed at the level of individual and group consciousness, blacks fashioned race into a cultural identity that resisted white hegemonic discourses.

The "two-ness" of being both American and Negro, which Du Bois so eloquently captured in 1903, resonates across time. If blacks as individuals referred to a divided subjectivity—"two warring ideals in one body"—they also spoke of a collective identity in the colonial terms of a "nation within a nation." The many and varied voices of black nationalism have resounded again and again from the earliest days of the American republic. Black nationalism found advocates in Paul Cuffee, John Russwurm, and Martin Delany in the nineteenth century, and Marcus Garvey, Malcolm X, and Stokely Carmichael in the twentieth. We know far too little about women's perceptions of nationalism, but Pauline Hopkins's serialized novel *Of One Blood* (1903) counterposes black and Anglo-Saxon races: "The dawn of the Twentieth century finds the Black race fighting for existence in every quarter of the globe. From over the sea Africa stretches her hands to the American Negro and cries aloud for sympathy in her hour of trial. . . . In America, caste prejudice has received fresh impetus as the 'Southern brother' of the Anglo-Saxon family has arisen from the ashes of secession, and like the prodigal of old, has been gorged with fatted calf and 'fixin's.'"

Likewise Hannah Nelson, an elementary school graduate employed most of her life in domestic service, told anthropologist John Langston Gwaltney in the 1970s: "We are a nation. The best of us have said it and everybody feels it. I know that will probably bother your white readers, but it is nonetheless true that black people think of themselves as an entity." Thus, when historian Barbara Fields observes that "Afro-Americans invented themselves, not as a race, but as a nation," she alludes to race as a double-voiced discourse. For blacks, race signified cultural identity and heritage, not biological inferiority. However, Fields's discussion understates the power of race to mean nation— specifically, race as the sign of perceived kinship ties between blacks in Africa and throughout the diaspora. In the crucible of the Middle Passage and American slavery, the multiple linguistic, tribal, and ethnic divisions among Africans came to be forged into a single, common ancestry. While not adhering to "scientific" explanations of superior and inferior races, African-Americans inscribed the black nation with racially laden meanings of blood ties that bespoke a lineage and culture more imagined than real.

"White Lines" from *White by Law: The Legal Construction of Race* (1996)

Ian Haney López

Working at the complex intersection of race, history, and law, Ian Haney López's scholarship is broad and far-reaching. In the following passage from White by Law: The Legal Construction of Race, *he argues that law—particularly Constitutional law and immigration law—is a political technology that creates and sustains the ideology of race.*

. . . This recognition of the role of law in the social dynamics of racial identity arguably lies near the heart of critical race theory. As John Calmore argues, "Critical race theory begins with a recognition that 'race' is not a fixed term. Instead, 'race' is a fluctuating, decentered complex of social meanings that are formed and transformed under the constant pressures of political struggle." Critical race theory increasingly acknowledges the extent to which race is not an independent given on which the law acts, but rather a social construction at least in part fashioned by law.

Despite the spreading recognition that law is a prime suspect in the formation of races, however, to date there has been no attempt to evaluate systematically just how the law creates and maintains races. How does the operation of law contribute to the formation of races? More particularly, by what mechanisms do courts and legislatures elaborate races, and what is the role of legal actors in these processes? Do legal rules construct races through the direct control of human behavior, or do they work more subtly as an ideology shaping our notions of what is and what can be? By the same token, are legal actors aware of their role in the fabrication of races, or are they unwitting participants, passive actors caught in processes beyond their ken and control? These are the questions this book attempts to answer. I suggest that law constructs races in a complex manner through both coercion and ideology, with legal actors as both conscious and unwitting participants. Rather than turning directly to theories of how law creates and maintains racial difference, however, I would like here to explore at greater length what is meant by the basic assertion that law constructs race.

A more precise definition of race will help us explore the importance of law in its creation. Race can be understood as the historically contingent social systems of meaning that attach to elements of morphology and ancestry. This definition can be pushed on three interrelated levels, the physical, the social, and the material. First, race turns on physical features and lines of descent, not because features or lineage themselves are a function of racial variation, but because society has invested these with racial meanings. Second, because the meanings given to certain features and ancestries denote race, it is the social processes of ascribing racialized meanings to faces and forbearers that lie at the heart of racial fabrication. Third, these meaning-systems, while originally only ideas, gain force as they are reproduced in the material conditions of society. The distribution of wealth and poverty turns in part on the actions of social and legal actors who have accepted ideas of race, with the resulting material conditions becoming part of and reinforcement for the contingent meanings understood as race.

Examining the role of law in the construction of race becomes, then, an examination of the possible ways in which law creates differences in physical appearance, of the extent to which law ascribes racialized meanings to physical features and ancestry, and of the ways in which law translates ideas about race into the material societal conditions that confirm and entrench those ideas.

Initially, it may be difficult to see how laws could possibly create differences in physical appearance. Biology, it seems, must be the sole provenance of morphology, while laws would appear to have no ability to regulate what people look like. However, laws have shaped the physical features evident in our society. While admittedly laws cannot alter the biology governing human morphology, rule-makers can and have altered the human behavior that produces variations in physical appearance. In other words, laws have directly shaped reproductive choices. The prerequisite laws evidence this on two levels. First, these laws constrained reproductive choices by excluding people with certain features from this country. From 1924 until the end of racial prerequisites to naturalization in 1952, persons ineligible for citizenship could not enter the United States. The prerequisite laws determined the types of faces and features present in the United States, and thus, who could marry and bear children here. Second, the prerequisite laws had a more direct regulatory reproductive effect through the legal consequences imposed on women who married noncitizen men. Until 1931, a woman could not naturalize if she was married to a foreigner racially ineligible for citizenship, even if she otherwise qualified to naturalize in every respect. Furthermore, women who were U.S. citizens were automatically stripped of their citizenship upon marriage to such a person. These legal penalties for marriage to racially barred aliens made such unions far less likely, and thus skewed the procreative choices that determined the appearance of the U.S. population. The prerequisite laws have directly shaped the physical appearance of people in the United States by limiting entrance to certain physical types and by altering the range of marital choices available to people here. What we look like, the literal and "racial" features we in this country exhibit, is to a large extent the product of legal rules and decisions.

Race is not, however, simply a matter of physical appearance and ancestry. Instead, it is primarily a function of the meanings given to these. On this level, too, law creates races. The statutes and cases that make up the laws of this country have directly contributed to defining the range of meanings without which notions of race could not exist. Recall the exclusion from citizenship of Ozawa and Thind. These cases established the significance of physical features on two levels. On the most obvious one, they established in stark terms the denotation and connotation of being non-White versus that of being White. To be the former meant one was unfit for naturalization, while to be the latter defined one as suited for citizenship. This stark division necessarily also carried important connotations regarding, for example, agency, will, moral authority, intelligence, and belonging. To be unfit for naturalization—that is, to be non-White—implied a certain degeneracy of intellect, morals, self-restraint, and political values; to be suited for citizenship—to be White—suggested moral maturity, self-assurance, personal independence, and political sophistication. These cases thus aided in the construction of the positive and negative meanings associated with racial difference, at least by giving such meanings legitimacy, and at most by actually fabricating them. The normative meanings that attach to racial difference— the contingent evaluations of worth, temperament, intellect, culture, and so on, which are at the core of racial beliefs—are partially the product of law.

"Punks, Bulldaggers, and Welfare Queens: The Radical Potential of Queer Politics?" (1997)

Cathy J. Cohen

Black feminist scholar and activist Cathy J. Cohen's work centers on Black politics, gender, queer studies, and social movement histories. Known for her work with the Black Youth Project—a nationwide survey that focuses on the lives of Black youths—she blends qualitative research with quantitative analysis to assess how Black youths make sense of (and overcome) political challenges. In Cohen's 1997 landmark essay "Punks, Bulldaggers, and Welfare Queens: The Radical Potential of Queer Politics?" she argues that "one of the great failings of queer theory and queer politics has been their inability to incorporate the roles that race, class, and gender play in defining people into analysis of the world and strategies for political mobilization."

. . . It is my argument, as I stated earlier, that one of the great failings of queer theory and especially queer politics has been their inability to incorporate into analysis of the world and strategies for political mobilization the roles that race, class, and gender play in defining people's diverging relations to dominant and normalizing power. I present this essay as the beginning of a much longer and protracted struggle to acknowledge and delineate the distribution of power within and outside of queer communities. This is a discussion of how to build a politics organized not merely by reductive categories of straight and queer, but organized instead around a more intersectional analysis of who and what the enemy is and where our potential allies can be found. This analysis seeks to make clear the privilege and power embedded in the categorizations of, on the one hand, an upstanding, "morally correct," white, state-authorized, middle-class, male *heterosexual*, and on the other, a culturally deficient, materially bankrupt, state dependent *heterosexual* woman of color, the latter found most often in our urban centers (those that haven't been gentrified), on magazine covers, and on the evening news.

I contend, therefore, that the radical potential of queer politics, or any liberatory movement, rests on its ability to advance strategically oriented political identities arising from a more nuanced understanding of power. One of the most difficult tasks in such an endeavor (and there are many) is not to forsake the complexities of both how power is structured and how we might think about the coalitions we create. Far too often movements revert to a position in which membership and joint political work are based on a necessarily similar history of oppression—but this is too much like identity politics. Instead, I am suggesting that the process of movement building be rooted not in our shared history or identity, but in our shared marginal relationship to dominant power which normalizes, legitimizes, and privileges.

We must, therefore, start our political work from the recognition that multiple systems of oppression are in operation and that these systems use institutionalized categories and identities to regulate and socialize. We must also understand that power and access to dominant resources are distributed across the boundaries of "het" and "queer" that we construct. A model of queer politics that simply pits the grand "heterosexuals" against all those oppressed "queers" is ineffectual as the basis for action in a political environment dominated by Newt Gingrich, the Christian Right, and the recurring ideology of white supremacy. As we stand on the verge of watching those in power dismantle the welfare system through a process of demonizing the poor and young, primarily poor and young women of color—many of whom have existed for their entire lives outside the white, middle-class heterosexual norm—we have to ask if these women do not fit into society's categories of marginal, deviant, and "queer." As we watch the explosion of prison construction and the disproportionate incarceration rates of young men and women of color, often as part of the economic development of poor white rural communities, we have to ask if these individuals do not fit society's definition of "queer" and expendable.

I am not proposing a political strategy that homogenizes and glorifies the experience of poor heterosexual people of color. In fact, in calling for a more expansive left political identity and formation I do not seek to erase the specific historical relation between the stigma of "queer" and the sexual activity of gay men, lesbians, bisexual, and transgendered individuals. And in no way do I intend or desire to equate the experiences of marginal heterosexual women and men to the lived experiences of queers. There is no doubt that heterosexuality, even for those heterosexuals who stand outside the norms of heteronormativity, results in some form of privilege and feelings of supremacy. I need only recount the times when other women of color, more economically vulnerable than myself, expressed superiority and some feelings of disgust when they realized that the nice young professor (me) was "that way."

However, in recognizing the distinct history of oppression that lesbian, gay, bisexual, and transgendered people have confronted and challenged, I am not willing to embrace every queer as my marginalized political ally. In the same way, I do not assume that shared racial, gender, and/or class position or identity guarantees or produces similar political commitments. Thus, identities and communities, while important to this strategy, must be complicated and destabilized through a recognition of the multiple social positions and relations to dominant power found *within* any one category or identity....

"Race: The Floating Signifier" (1997)

Stuart Hall

Known for pushing the fields of cultural studies and Black Studies toward a deeper consideration of diaspora, Stuart Hall (1932–2014) was a Jamaican British scholar, writer, and cultural critic. Perhaps best known for his 1978 book Policing the Crisis: Mugging, the State, and Law and Order, *Hall offers a landmark study on the production of racialized notions of "crime" through the framework of moral panics and institutional responses to them. As a noted theoretician of race, Hall makes the case in the following lightly edited excerpt from "Race: The Floating Signifier" that race is a political construction and has no basis in biology.*

In human culture, I would say, the propensity to classify sub-groups of human types; to break up the diversity of human society into very distinct typings according to essentialized characteristics, whether physical characteristics or intellectual ones, or characteristics of the body and so on this a very profound kind of cultural impulse. In a way, it's a very positive cultural impulse because we now understand the importance of all forms of classification to meaning. Until you can classify things, in different ways, you can't generate any meaning at all. So, it's an absolutely fundamental aspect of human culture. What is, of course, important for us is when the systems of classification become the objects of the disposition of power. That's to say when the marking of difference and similarity across a human population becomes a reason why this group is to be treated in that way and get those advantages, and that group should be treated in another. It's the coming together of difference, or categorization of our classification and power. The use of classification as a system of power, which is really what is very profound and one then sees that across a range of different characteristics. You see it in gender, the ascription of clear masculine and feminine identities and the assumption from that that you can predict whole ranges of behavior and aspirations and opportunities from this classification. Classification is a very generative thing once you are classified a whole range of other things fall into place as a result of it. But, another important point about classification is that it . . . is a way of maintaining the order of any system, and what is most disturbing is that anything that breaks the classification. So, you know, it's not just that you have blacks and whites, but of course one group of those people have a much more positive value than the other group. That's how power operates. But then, anything that attempts to ascribe to the black population, characteristics that used to be used for the white ones, generates enormous tension in the society. Mary Douglas, the anthropologist, describes this in terms of what she calls "matter out of place." She says every culture has a kind of order of classification built into it and this seems to stabilize the culture. You know exactly where you are, you know who are the inferiors and who the superiors are and how each has a rank, etc. What disturbs you is what she calls "matter out of place." What she means by that is you don't worry about dirt in the garden because it belongs in the garden but the moment you see dirt in the bedroom you have to do something about it because it doesn't symbolically belong there. And what you do with dirt in the bedroom is you cleanse it, you sweep it out, you restore the order, you police the boundaries, you know the hard and fixed boundaries between what belongs and what doesn't. Inside/outside. Cultured/uncivilized. Barbarous and cultivated, and so on.

And races, of course, one of the principle forms of human classification, which have all of these negative and positive attributes kind of built into it. So, in a way, they function as a common sense code in our society. So, in a way, you don't need to have a whole argument, you know, about "are blacks intelligent?" The moment you say that blacks, already the equivalences begin to trip off peoples mind. Blacks then, sound bodies, good at sports, good at dancing, very expressive, no intelligence, never had a thought in their heads, you know, tendency to barbarous behavior. All these things are clustered, simply in the classification system itself. What I'm interested in then is how these definitions of race come to operate, how they function. I'm interested partly of how they function, of course, in the systems of classification, which are used in order to divide populations into different ethnic or racial groups and to ascribe characteristics to these different groupings and to assume a kind of normal behavior or conduct about them. Because they are this kind of person, they can do that sort of thing, and we'll believe that sort of thing, and we'll suffer from that set of problems, etc. Everything is kind of inscribed in their species being, their very being because of their race. So, I think that ones seeing there is a kind of essentializing of race and a whole range of, diverse range of characteristics ultimately fixed or held in place because people have been categorized in a certain way, racially.

These are very big cultural principals we're talking about and a whole lot in terms of power and exclusion results from having the system of classification. So, . . . I want to talk about how this, how race as a principal of classification operates to sort out the world into its superiors and inferiors along some line of biological or genetic race and how as a consequence of that all the conduct of society towards black people is inflicted and shaped by that system of classification.

I end the lecture with the phrase, "politics without guarantees," and what I mean by that is . . . if you think that race is a fixed biological characteristic, and that a whole number of other things: cultural qualities, intellectual qualities, emotional and expressive qualities follow from the fact of being genetically one race or another, if that is your image of race. You will think, then, that the very fact of race can actually guarantee a whole range of things including . . . whether the works of art produced by a person who biologically belongs to that race is good or not. So, you know, if they're black it means that they're also very expressive, it also means they'll produce a certain kind of work of art and it'll be good because it's black. And similarly, a certain kind of politics that defends the race, tries to protect us against discrimination, etc. In which all black people will be figured as people who are holding the correct position and when you ask what positions do they hold what you will respond is not the normal political argument: "Well they believe in the following things which I think are viable and progressive things for black people to vie for now in order to change their circumstances." You will say well they're like that, they think like that because that's how black people think, it's right that black people should—. So it's right that these functions act as a kind of guarantee that the work of art will be good because it's black and will be politically progressive because it's black. Now, we actually know that the [work] does not come out like that. Some of the [works] are not good. Though black, made with the best of positive intentions to reverse negative stereotypes, to praise the diversity of black people, they just don't work aesthetically. And similarly, we know black people have a range of different political positions: conservative, reactionary, progressive, and so on. And that these fall out in a way in which is not defined by their genetic or biological disposition. So, I'm trying to end the notion that our politics is to cure. We know it's correct entering the very, very difficult debate. Are we correct? What is the right strategy now? What are the tactics we ought to adopt? Who can we be in alliances with? What is the strategic thing, in this moment, to go for? You know, the normal game of politics. It sort of in a way prevents us from having to play that difficult game because we have another guarantee. We know it is because we wrote it and I think in a way it leads to a kind of mechanistic anti-racist politics—not a thoughtful one, not a self critical one, not a reflexive one. So, by ending the guarantee, I don't mean by that of course that it's black people or black politics that's involved. The reason why it matters is not because what's in our genes it's because of what is in our history. It's because black people have been in a certain position in society, in history, over a long period of time that those are the conditions they're in and that's what they're fighting against. And of course that matters, but then black, the term black, is referring to this long history of political and historical oppression. It's not referring to our genes. It's not referring to our biology. And in order to fight a politics, which is effective in ending the oppression of black people, you have to ask what is the right politics to do. You can't depend on the fact that it's blacks doing it; that this will guarantee in heaven that you're doing the right thing. So I want blacks to enter into what I think they've been reserved in doing, which is, you know the hard graft of having arguments with their own fellows, men and women who are black, about it. And that's a difficult thing because in a way you have to mobilize effectively, you can't depend on just the race to take you to your political objective. And it's not therefore that I have a counter-politic to the existing politics of racism to put into the space but it's rather a sort of approach to the political which I always see as not a practice which has any guarantees built into it, it's not, there is no law of history which tells you we will win, we may lose. Just as there is no law of history, which will [mean] human beings won't blow themselves to bits, they probably will. So one has to act in the notion that politics is always open. It's always the contingent of failure and you need to be right because there is no guarantee except good practice to make it right to mobilization, to having the right people on your side committed to the program. So I want people to take politics a bit more seriously and to take biology less seriously.

"Color Blindness, History, and the Law"
from *The House That Race Built* (1997)

Kimberlé Crenshaw

Kimberlé Crenshaw is a legal scholar and cultural critic known for coining the term "intersectionality" and being an early exponent of critical race theory. Her contributions to the field of law have been astonishingly broad and consequential. In the excerpt below from her article "Color Blindness, History, and the Law," Crenshaw argues that the law is a reflection of how the state chooses to exert its power over people through legal and ideological constructions of race.

It is fairly obvious that treating different things the same can generate as much an inequality as treating the same things differently. Anatole France captured that inequality when he noted that the law in its majestic equality prevents the rich and the poor from sleeping under bridges. Clearly, the law works in inequality when the rich will never seek that worldly pleasure, and the poor have no other choice. A similar denial of social power differentials between racial groups reproduces and insulates that very power disparity. Formal equality in conditions of social inequality becomes a tool of domination, reinforcing that system and insulating it from attack....

Just as the realists showed that there was in fact no free market, much of critical race theory is attempting to show that there is no free market of race that determines relationships between blacks and whites. There is no free competition between blacks and whites in part because the law actually structures those relationships across a wide range of societal competitions over certain social resources.

To conclude, the doctrine of color blindness, along with the nine-teenth-century market vision it endorses, uses and redeploys in the context of equal opportunity very narrow visions of equality and a specific contested vision of the notion of the private sphere. It not only works to legitimize material deprivations, but it also produces a particular ideological regime. That regime forces African Americans into articulating legitimate demands within the discourse of victimhood. Doing so is the only way that blacks can achieve political power: to show that there is a defect in the market and that the defect is constituted by an intentional, particular, state actor articulating its decision to discriminate solely on the basis of skin color—that is, essentially forcing black people to articulate themselves as perfect victims as against a perfect discriminator. Consequentially, when blacks are told that they should not be deploying the use of victimology as a way of articulating demands, they are essentially being forced into a catch-22. The only way one can achieve political power through this structure is to articulate ourselves as victims, yet the very articulation of ourselves as victims is a justification for rejecting our claim. In the law, it is clear that the end of interpretation is usually the exercise of state power. Such interpretation is produced by the ways state power, in fact, will be deployed in a particular context.

I think we need to be prepared to understand the distributive consequences of legal ideology, particularly legal ideology that produces social discourses of victimhood, and to reject the invisibility of law in structuring those discourses. In race matters, I think we need to be prepared relentlessly to show how, in fact, law matters.

"Introduction: Black Studies and the Racial Mountain"

from *Dispatches from the Ebony Tower* (2000)

Manning Marable

Manning Marable's (1950–2011) work has been indispensable to the field of Black Studies. From his writings on Malcolm X to his trenchant 1983 classic How Capitalism Underdeveloped Black America, *Marable's scholarship explores the relationship between Black liberation, social movement histories, and Black Studies. In the excerpt below from "Black Studies and the Racial Mountain," Marable argues that the Black intellectual tradition—and therefore Black Studies—"can be characterized by three great points of departure": descriptive, corrective, and prescriptive.*

Behind the concept of African American studies is essentially the black intellectual tradition, the critical thought and perspectives of intellectuals of African descent and scholars of black America, and Africa, and the black diaspora. That black intellectual tradition can be characterized by three great points of departure. First, the black intellectual tradition has always been descriptive, that is, presenting the reality of black life and experiences from the point of view of black people themselves. Instead of beginning the logic of intellectual inquiry standing on the outside of the lived experiences of the people, the black intellectual tradition at its best has always presumed the centrality of black life. The scholar was a participant-observer who was challenged to undertake a thick description of cultural and social phenomena. Scholarship was therefore grounded in the very subjective truths of a people's collective experience. It is from this experience that historical knowledge can be constructed that accurately describes and defines the contours of consciousness and identity.

The black intellectual tradition has, second, been corrective. It has attempted to challenge and to critique the racism and stereotypes that have been ever present in the mainstream discourse of white academic institutions. Our intellectual tradition has vigorously condemned and disputed theories of black people's genetic, biological, and cultural inferiority. It has attacked the distorted representation of blackness found in the dominant culture. It has challenged Eurocentric notions of aesthetics and beauty that, all too often, are grounded in an implied, or even explicit, contempt for the standards of blackness.

And, finally, the black intellectual tradition has been prescriptive. Black scholars who have theorized from the black experience have often proposed practical steps for the empowerment of black people. In other words, there is a practical connection between scholarship and struggle, between social analysis and social transformation. The purpose of black scholarship is more than the restoration of identity and self-esteem: it is to use history and culture as tools through which people interpret their collective experience, but for the purpose of transforming their actual conditions and the totality of the society all around them. This common recognition of the broad social purpose of intellectual work did not mean that black scholarship must be a kind of narrow advocacy or a partisan polemic with no genuine standards of objectivity. Black scholars within the classical tradition placed great emphasis on their methodologies and fostered rigorous approaches to the collection and interpretation of data. But the high standards they sought to maintain, despite their woefully inadequate research funding and material resources, did not contradict their belief that new knowledge could in some way serve and empower those people with whom they shared a common culture, heritage, and struggle. Thus black studies was never simply the scholarship of intellectuals who just happened to be black, nor was it the research about the black experience by just anyone of any random ethnic background and ideological bias. Black studies was never a subcategory of some race-based ideology but a critical body of scholarship that sought over time to dismantle powerful racist intellectual categories and white supremacy itself.

"Venus in Two Acts" (2008)

Saidiya Hartman

Saidiya Hartman's work defies easy characterization in its breadth, creativity, and rigor. Centering fields of interest such as African American and American literature, cultural history, law and literature, slavery, and performance studies, she has published field-defining titles like Scenes of Subjection: Terror, Slavery, and Self-Making in Nineteenth-Century America *(1997) and* Lose Your Mother: A Journey along the Atlantic Slave Route *(2006). The passage below is from Hartman's essay "Venus in Two Acts" and offers a meditation on how one ethically narrates the counterhistories of slavery and what kind of stories can be told by and about those "who live in such an intimate relationship with death."*

How can narrative embody life in words and at the same time respect what we cannot know? How does one listen for the groans and cries, the undecipherable songs, the crackle of fire in the cane fields, the laments for the dead, and the shouts of victory, and then assign words to all of it? Is it possible to construct a story from "the locus of impossible speech" or resurrect lives from the ruins? Can beauty provide an antidote to dishonor, and love a way to "exhume buried cries" and reanimate the dead?

Or is narration its own gift and its own end, that is, all that is realizable when overcoming the past and redeeming the dead are not? And what do stories afford anyway? A way of living in the world in the aftermath of catastrophe and devastation? A home in the world for the mutilated and violated self? For whom—for us or for them?

The scarcity of African narratives of captivity and enslavement exacerbate the pressure and gravity of such questions. There is not one extant autobiographical narrative of a female captive who survived the Middle Passage. This silence in the archive in combination with the robustness of the fort or barracoon, not as a holding cell or space of confinement but as an episteme, has for the most part focused the historiography of the slave trade on quantitative matters and on issues of markets and trade relations. Loss gives rise to longing, and in these circumstances, it would not be far-fetched to consider stories as a form of compensation or even as reparations, perhaps the only kind we will ever receive.

As a writer committed to telling stories, I have endeavored to represent the lives of the nameless and the forgotten, to reckon with loss, and to respect the limits of what cannot be known. For me, narrating counter-histories of slavery has always been inseparable from writing a history of present, by which I mean the incomplete project of freedom, and the precarious life of the ex-slave, a condition defined by the vulnerability to premature death and to gratuitous acts of violence. As I understand it, a history of the present strives to illuminate the intimacy of our experience with the lives of the dead, to write our now as it is interrupted by this past, and to imagine a *free state*, not as the time before captivity or slavery, but rather as the anticipated future of this writing.

This writing is personal because this history has engendered me, because "the knowledge of the other marks me," because of the pain experienced in my encounter with the scraps of the archive, and because of the kinds of stories I have fashioned to bridge the past and the present and to dramatize the production of nothing—empty rooms, and silence, and lives reduced to waste.

What are the kinds of stories to be told by those and about those who live in such an intimate relationship with death? Romances? Tragedies? Shrieks that find their way into speech and song? What are the protocols and limits that shape the narratives written as counter-history, an aspiration that isn't a prophylactic against the risks posed by reiterating violent speech and depicting again rituals of torture? How does one revisit the scene of subjection without replicating the grammar of violence? Is the "terrible beauty" that resides in such a scene something akin to remedy as Fred Moten would seem to suggest? The kind of terrible beauty and terrible music that he discerns in Aunt Hester's screams transformed into the songs of the Great House Farm or in the photograph of Emmett Till's destroyed face, and the "acuity of regard," which arises from a willingness to look into the open casket. Do the possibilities outweigh the dangers of looking (again)?

"Conclusion: The Conundrum of Criminality" from *The Condemnation of Blackness: Race, Crime, and the Making of Modern Urban America* (2010)

Khalil Gibran Muhammad

Scholar of racism, economic inequality, criminal justice, and democracy in US history, Khalil Gibran Muhammad writes at the intersection of race and its connection to criminalization, freedom, and public policy. In his book The Condemnation of Blackness: Race, Crime, and the Making of Modern Urban America, *excerpted below, he argues that the very idea of "Black criminality" was central to how freedom—particularly white freedom—was conceptualized and acted upon in the making of the nineteenth- and twentieth-century urban United States.*

The idea of black criminality was crucial to the making of modern urban America. In nearly every sphere of life it impacted how people defined fundamental differences between native whites, immigrants, and blacks. It also impacted, by comparison, how people evaluated black people's presence—the Negro Problem, as it had once been called—in the urban North. In education, in housing, in jobs, in leisure and recreation, the idea shaped the "public transcript" of the modern urban world. Moreover, the various ways in which writers and reformers imagined black people as inferior to and fundamentally different from native whites and immigrants in the early twentieth century had a direct impact on the allocation of social resources for preventing crime in all communities, with the smallest amount flowing to black communities. Native whites and immigrants were much more likely to benefit directly from the most thoughtful and forward-thinking (or progressive) social work and social science during the early twentieth century. Regardless of whether one views Americanization programs as an attempt to strip European immigrants of their language, religion, and cultural institutions, the impetus grew out of a desire to eradicate differences rather than to accentuate them. Social workers and settlement house reformers were active agents in the effort to assimilate immigrants into American culture and society. They did not leave immigrants to work out their own salvation, though some immigrants tried mightily to disrupt these plans with their fierce attachment to cultural traditions and institutions derived from their homelands. Long before the latemodel black drug dealer became public enemy number one, white bootleggers, drug pushers, pimps, common thieves, and thugs plied their trade in black communities alongside their black peers, but with the police on their side. Thoughtful, well funded crime prevention and politically accountable crime fighting secured immigrants' whiteness, in contrast to the experiences of blacks, who were often brutalized or left unprotected and were repeatedly told to conquer their own crime before others would help them.

The destructive consequences of the black crime discourse went beyond limited reform efforts in black communities; it also limited the application of pioneering sociological concepts to record and interpret the black experience. As much as progressives used statistical knowledge and social surveys as part of their arsenal of knowledge about immigrant inequality, they did not use data to shame immigrants into respectable behavior. Progressives used crime statistics to demonstrate the suffering of poor and working-class immigrants and native whites. They frequently rejected the data as "too statistical" because it submerged the humanity of the people and masked the "aggravating causes" of crime. The decriminalization of immigrants by progressives decades before the New Deal drew on immigrant crime statistics as an index of their assimilability—as "Americans in Process"—and of both their economic, social, and political oppression. This was the choice progressives made to bring immigrants into the fold of American life. For these reformers, immigrants' humanity trumped the scale of their crimes and the cultural expressions of their social resistance.

By contrast, African American crime to many white race-relations experts stood as an almost singular reflection of black culture and humanity. For these writers, anything less than a full-throttle use of black crime statistics was deemed "too sentimental," too soft on crime. Downplaying the statistics, they often claimed, was no more than a biased attempt to conceal the dangerous criminal tendencies of the Negro stranger in America's midst. . . .

By illuminating the idea of black criminality in the making of modern urban America, it becomes clear that there are options in how we choose to use and interpret crime statistics. They may tell us something about the world we live in and about the people we label "criminals." But they cannot tell us everything. Far from it. For good or for bad, the numbers do not speak for themselves. They never have. They have always been interpreted, and made meaningful, in a broader political, economic, and social context in which race mattered. The falsity of past claims of race neutral crime statistics and color-blind justice should caution us against the ubiquitous referencing of statistics about black criminality today, especially given the relative silence about white criminality. The invisible layers of racial ideology packed into the statistics, sociological theories, and the everyday stories we continue to tell about crime in modern urban America are a legacy of the past. The choice about which narratives we attach to the data in the future, however, is ours to make. . . .

"Introduction" from

The New Jim Crow: Mass Incarceration in the Age of Colorblindness (2010)

Michelle Alexander

Perhaps most well known for her bestselling book The New Jim Crow: Mass Incarceration in the Age of Colorblindness, *Michelle Alexander is a legal scholar, civil rights lawyer, and writer. In the excerpt below from* The New Jim Crow, *Alexander contends that the US government's genocidal, anti-Black "War on Drugs" served as one of the most significant factors in the hyperincarceration of Black people since the 1970s and argues that "the racial dimension of mass incarceration is its most striking feature."*

Most people assume the War on Drugs was launched in response to the crisis caused by crack cocaine in inner-city neighborhoods. This view holds that the racial disparities in drug convictions and sentences, as well as the rapid explosion of the prison population, reflect nothing more than the government's zealous—but benign—efforts to address rampant drug crime in poor, minority neighborhoods. This view, while understandable, given the sensational media coverage of crack in the 1980s and 1990s, is simply wrong.

While it is true that the publicity surrounding crack cocaine led to a dramatic increase in funding for the drug war (as well as to sentencing policies that greatly exacerbated racial disparities in incarceration rates), there is no truth to the notion that the War on Drugs was launched in response to crack co-caine. President Ronald Reagan officially announced the current drug war in 1982, before crack became an issue in the media or a crisis in poor black neigh-borhoods. A few years after the drug war was declared, crack began to spread rapidly in the poor black neighborhoods of Los Angeles and later emerged in cities across the country. The Reagan administration hired staff to publicize the emergence of crack cocaine in 1985 as part of a strategic effort to build public and legislative support for the war. The media campaign was an extraordinary success. Almost overnight, the media was saturated with images of black "crack whores," "crack dealers," and "crack babies"—images that seemed to confirm the worst negative racial stereotypes about impoverished inner-city residents. The media bonanza surrounding the "new demon drug" helped to catapult the War on Drugs from an ambitious federal policy to an actual war.

The timing of the crack crisis helped to fuel conspiracy theories and gener-al speculation in poor black communities that the War on Drugs was part of a genocidal plan by the government to destroy black people in the United States. From the outset, stories circulated on the street that crack and other drugs were being brought into black neighborhoods by the CIA. Eventually, even the Ur-ban League came to take the claims of genocide seriously. In its 1990 report "The State of Black America," it stated: "There is at least one concept that must be recognized if one is to see the pervasive and insidious nature of the drug problem for the African American community. Though difficult to accept, that is the concept of genocide." While the conspiracy theories were initially dis-missed as far-fetched, if not downright loony, the word on the street turned out to be right, at least to a point. The CIA admitted in 1998 that guerilla armies it actively supported in Nicaragua were smuggling illegal drugs into the United States—drugs that were making their way onto the streets of inner-city black neighborhoods in the form of crack cocaine. The CIA also admitted that, in the midst of the War on Drugs, it blocked law enforcement efforts to investigate illegal drug networks that were helping to fund its covert war in Nicaragua.

It bears emphasis that the CIA never admitted (nor has any evidence been revealed to support the claim) that it intentionally sought the destruction of the black community by allowing illegal drugs to be smuggled into the United States. Nonetheless, conspiracy theorists surely must be forgiven for their bold accusa-tion of genocide, in light of the devastation wrought by crack cocaine and the drug war, and the odd coincidence that an illegal drug crisis suddenly appeared in the black community after—not before—a drug war had been declared. In fact, the War on Drugs began at a time when illegal drug use was on the decline. During this same time period, however, a war was declared, causing arrests and convictions for drug offenses to skyrocket, especially among people of color.

The impact of the drug war has been astounding. In less than thirty years, the U.S. penal population exploded from around 300,000 to more than 2 million, with drug convictions accounting for the majority of the increase. The United States now has the highest rate of incarceration in the world, dwarfing the rates of nearly every developed country, even surpassing those in highly repressive regimes like Russia, China, and Iran. In Germany, 93 people are in prison for every 100,000 adults and children. In the United States, the rate is roughly eight times that, or 750 per 100,000.

The racial dimension of mass incarceration is its most striking feature. No other country in the world imprisons so many of its racial or ethnic minorities. The United States imprisons a larger percentage of its black population than South Africa did at the height of apartheid. In Washington, D.C., our nation's capital, it is estimated that three out of four young black men (and nearly all those in the poorest neighborhoods) can expect to serve time in prison. Similar rates of incarceration can be found in black communities across America.

These stark racial disparities cannot be explained by rates of drug crime. Studies show that people of all colors *use and sell* illegal drugs at remarkably similar rates. If there are significant differences in the surveys to be found, they frequently suggest that whites, particularly white youth, are more likely to engage in drug crime than people of color. That is not what one would guess, however, when entering our nation's prisons and jails, which are overflowing with black and brown drug offenders. In some states, black men have been admitted to prison on drug charges at rates twenty to fifty times greater than those of white men. And in major cities wracked by the drug war, as many as 80 percent of young African American men now have criminal records and are thus subject to legalized discrimination for the rest of their lives. These young men are part of a growing undercaste, permanently locked up and locked out of mainstream society.

"The Case for Reparations" (2014)

Ta-Nehisi Coates

Ta-Nehisi Coates is an internationally known author, journalist, and cultural critic whose prolific work examines the relationship between US democracy, white supremacy, and Black life. In 2014, his widely read essay "The Case for Reparations" helped to put the idea of reparations back on the table as a matter of urgent national discussion. In the excerpt below, Coates argues that reparations would help to close the Black-white wealth gap and begin a material reckoning with the long and ongoing legacy of slavery in the United States.

The lives of black Americans are better than they were half a century ago. The humiliation of WHITES ONLY signs are gone. Rates of black poverty have decreased. Black teen-pregnancy rates are at record lows—and the gap between black and white teen-pregnancy rates has shrunk significantly. But such progress rests on a shaky foundation, and fault lines are everywhere. The income gap between black and white households is roughly the same today as it was in 1970. Patrick Sharkey, a sociologist at New York University, studied children born from 1955 through 1970 and found that 4 percent of whites and 62 percent of blacks across America had been raised in poor neighborhoods. A generation later, the same study showed, virtually nothing had changed. And whereas whites born into affluent neighborhoods tended to remain in affluent neighborhoods, blacks tended to fall out of them.

This is not surprising. Black families, regardless of income, are significantly less wealthy than white families. The Pew Research Center estimates that white households are worth roughly twenty times as much as black households, and that whereas only 15 percent of whites have zero or negative wealth, more than a third of blacks do. Effectively, the black family in America is working without a safety net. When financial calamity strikes—a medical emergency, divorce, job loss—the fall is precipitous.

And just as black families of all incomes remain handicapped by a lack of wealth, so too do they remain handicapped by their restricted choice of neighborhood. Black people with upper-middle-class incomes do not generally live in upper-middle-class neighborhoods. Sharkey's research shows that black families making $100,000 typically live in the kinds of neighborhoods inhabited by white families making $30,000. "Blacks and whites inhabit such different neighborhoods," Sharkey writes, "that it is not possible to compare the economic outcomes of black and white children."

A national real-estate association advised not to sell to "a colored man of means who was giving his children a college education."

The implications are chilling. As a rule, poor black people do not work their way out of the ghetto—and those who do often face the horror of watching their children and grandchildren tumble back.

Even seeming evidence of progress withers under harsh light. In 2012, the Manhattan Institute cheerily noted that segregation had declined since the 1960s. And yet African Americans still remained—by far—the most segregated ethnic group in the country.

With segregation, with the isolation of the injured and the robbed, comes the concentration of disadvantage. An unsegregated America might see poverty, and all its effects, spread across the country with no particular bias toward skin color. Instead, the concentration of poverty has been paired with a concentration of melanin. The resulting conflagration has been devastating. . . .

Scholars have long discussed methods by which America might make reparations to those on whose labor and exclusion the country was built. In the 1970s, the Yale Law professor Boris Bittker argued in *The Case for Black Reparations* that a rough price tag for reparations could be determined by multiplying the number of African Americans in the population by the difference in white and black per capita income. That number—$34 billion in 1973, when Bittker wrote his book—could be added to a reparations program each year for a decade or two. Today Charles Ogletree, the Harvard Law School professor, argues for something broader: a program of job training and public works that takes racial justice as its mission but includes the poor of all races.

To celebrate freedom and democracy while forgetting America's origins in a slavery economy is patriotism à la carte.

Perhaps no statistic better illustrates the enduring legacy of our country's shameful history of treating black people as sub-citizens, sub-Americans, and sub-humans than the wealth gap. Reparations would seek to close this chasm. But as surely as the creation of the wealth gap required the cooperation of every aspect of the society, bridging it will require the same.

"Black Study, Black Struggle" (2016)

Robin D. G. Kelley

Robin D. G. Kelley is a historian of social movements in the US, the African diaspora, and Africa, as well as Black intellectual genealogies and music and visual culture. Kelley has been a vocal defender of Black Studies and has written extensively on its development as a field of knowledge and inquiry. In "Black Study, Black Struggle," excerpted below, he argues that Black study and struggle for a liberated future must begin with love and a commitment to "advance the movements in the streets, seeking to eliminate racism and state violence, preserve black life, defend the rights of the marginalized (from undocumented immigrants to transfolk), and challenge the current order that has brought us so much misery."

Black studies was conceived not just outside the university but in opposition to a Eurocentric university culture with ties to corporate and military power. Having emerged from mass revolt, insurgent black studies scholars developed institutional models based in, but largely independent of, the academy. In later decades, these institutions were—with varying degrees of eagerness—incorporated into the university proper in response to pressure to embrace multiculturalism.

In 1969 Vincent Harding, Stephen Henderson, Abdul Alkalimat, A. B. Spellman, Larry Rushing, and Council Taylor founded the Institute of the Black World (IBW) at Atlanta University in order to mobilize the "collective scholarship" of black intellectuals to confront racism and colonialism, here and abroad. Black students, artists, and activists at the University of Chicago founded the Communiversity, offering courses in African history and Marxist political economy to community members on Chicago's South Side. Less than two decades later, the United Coalition Against Racism, a student organization at the University of Michigan, established the Ella Baker – Nelson Mandela Center for Anti-Racist Education (BMC). The center was never conceived as a safe space for students of color but rather as a resource for anti-racist struggles "dedicated to the principle of thinking in order to act." The BMC offered leadership training, sponsored cultural and educational events, provided rare anti-racist literature, and served as a radical place for study and critical engagement open to everyone, especially nonuniversity working-class residents.

In fact, it was during a talk held at IBW that the Guyanese historian Walter Rodney, some six years before he was martyred, urged radical black scholars to become "guerrilla intellectuals." By this he meant freeing ourselves from the "Babylonian captivity" of bourgeois society, moving beyond disciplinary imperatives, and "grounding" with the people so as to engage, act, and think collectively in terms of social movements. . . .

Taped inside the top drawer of my desk is a small scrap of paper with three words scrawled across it: "Love, Study, Struggle." It serves as a daily reminder of what I am supposed to be doing. Black study and resistance must begin with love. James Baldwin understood love-as-agency probably better than anyone. For him it meant to love ourselves as black *people*; it meant making love the motivation for making revolution; it meant envisioning a society where everyone is embraced, where there is no oppression, where every life is valued—even those who may once have been our oppressors. It *did not* mean seeking white people's love and acceptance or seeking belonging in the world created by our oppressor. In *The Fire Next Time* (1963), he is unequivocal: "I do not know many Negroes who are eager to be 'accepted' by white people, still less to be loved by them; they, the blacks, simply don't wish to be beaten over the head by the whites every instant of our brief passage on this planet." But here is the catch: if we are committed to genuine freedom, we have no choice but to love all. To love all is to fight relentlessly to end exploitation and oppression everywhere, even on behalf of those who think they hate us. This was Baldwin's point—perhaps his most misunderstood and reviled point.

To love this way requires relentless struggle, deep study, and critique. Limiting our ambit to suffering, resistance, and achievement is not enough. We must go to the root—the historical, political, social, cultural, ideological, material, economic root—of oppression in order to understand its negation, the prospect of our liberation. Going to the root illuminates what is hidden from us, largely because most structures of oppression and all of their various entanglements are simply not visible and not felt. For example, if we argue that state violence is merely a manifestation of anti-blackness because that is what we *see and feel*, we are left with no theory of the state and have no way of understanding racialized police violence in places such as Atlanta and Detroit, where most cops are black, unless we turn to some metaphysical explanation.

For my generation, the formal classroom was never the space for deep critique precisely because it was not a place of love. The classroom was—and still is—a performative space, where faculty and students compete with each other. Through study groups, we created our own intellectual communities held together by principle and love, though the specters of sectarianism, ego, and just-plain childishness blurred our vision and threatened our camaraderie. Still, the political study group was our lifeblood—both on and off campus. We lived by Karl Marx's pithy 1844 statement:

> But if the designing of the future and the proclamation of ready-made solutions for all time is not our affair, then we realize all the more clearly what we have to accomplish in the present—I am speaking of a ruthless criticism of everything existing, ruthless in two senses: The criticism must not be afraid of its own conclusions, nor of conflict with the powers that be.

Study groups introduced me to C. L. R. James, Frantz Fanon, Walter Rodney, Barbara Smith, Angela Davis, Karl Marx, Friedrich Engels, Vladimir Lenin, Chancellor Williams, George E. M. James, Shulamith Firestone, Kwame Nkrumah, Kwame Turé, Rosa Luxemburg, Antonio Gramsci, Chinweizu Ibekwe, Amílcar Cabral, and others. These texts were our sources of social critique and weapons in our class war on the bourgeois canon. As self-styled activist-intellectuals, it never occurred to us to *refuse* to read a text simply because it validated the racism, sexism, free-market ideology, and bourgeois liberalism against which we railed. Nothing was off limits. On the contrary, delving into these works only sharpened our critical faculties.

Love and study cannot exist without struggle, and struggle cannot occur solely inside the refuge we call the university. Being grounded in the world we wish to make is fundamental. As I argued in *Freedom Dreams* nearly fifteen years ago, "Social movements generate new knowledge, new theories, new questions. The most radical ideas often grow out of a concrete intellectual engagement with the problems of aggrieved populations confronting systems of oppression." Ironically I wrote these words with my students in mind, many of whom were involved in campus struggles, feeling a bit rudderless but believing that the only way to make themselves into authentic activists was to leave the books and radical theories at home or in their dorms. The undercommons offers students a valuable model of study that takes for granted the indivisibility of thought and struggle, not unlike its antecedent, the Mississippi Freedom Schools.

The Mississippi Freedom Schools, initially launched by the Student Non-Violent Coordinating Committee as part of the 1964 Freedom Summer, were intended to create "an educational experience for students which will make it possible for them to challenge the myths of our society, to perceive more clearly its realities and to find alternatives, and ultimately, new directions for action." The curriculum included traditional subjects that publicly funded black schools did not offer, but they were never designed to be simply *better* versions of the traditional liberal education model. Rather, students examined power along the axes of race and class. Students and teachers worked together to reveal how ruling whites profited from Jim Crow, and they included in their analysis the precarious position of poor whites. Rural black kids of all ages learned to distinguish between "Material Things and Soul Things," developing a trenchant critique of materialism. The freedom schools challenged the myth that the civil rights movement was just about claiming a place in mainstream society. They didn't want equal opportunity in a burning house; they wanted to build a new house.

Perhaps one of the best historical models of radical, collective, grounded intellectual work was launched by black feminists Patricia Robinson, Patricia Haden, and Donna Middleton, working with community residents of Mt. Vernon, New York, many of whom were unemployed, low-wage workers, welfare mothers, and children. Together, they organized and read as a community—from elders to children. They saw education as a vehicle for collective transformation and an incubator of knowledge, not a path to upward mobility and material wealth. Influenced by Frantz Fanon, they interrogated and critiqued racism, sexism, slavery, and capitalism, emphasizing the ways in which racism produced a kind of psychosis among poor black people. Their study and activism culminated in a collectively written, independently published book called *Lessons from the Damned* (1973). It is a remarkable book, with essays by adults as well as children—some as young as twelve, who developed trenchant criticisms of public school teachers and the education system.

Although they acknowledged the unavoidability of addressing trauma, they understood that one's activism could not stop there. In a section titled "The Revolt of Poor Black Women," the authors insisted that a genuine revolution requires the overthrow of capitalism, the elimination of male supremacy, and the transformation of self. Revolution, they argued, is supposed to usher in a brand new beginning; it is driven by the power of freed imagination, not the dead weight of the past. As Robinson, Haden, and Middleton wrote, "All revolutionaries, regardless of sex, are the smashers of myths and the destroyers of illusion. They have always died and lived again to build new myths. They dare to dream of a utopia, a new kind of synthesis and equilibrium."

At UCLA, where I teach, these same insights are taking a new form. A group of graduate students launched their version of the undercommons in January 2016. Based on the Freedom School model, UCLA's undercommons holds weekly outdoor meetings featuring activists from groups such as Black Lives Matter, Critical Resistance, and the L.A. Poverty Department. Faculty and students lead discussions. These events have drawn as many as 150 students, and the community continues to grow. The primary organizers—Thabisile Griffin, Marques Vestal, Olúfẹ́mi O. Táíwò, Sa Whitley, and Shamell Bell—are all doctoral students who see the university as a site of contestation, a place of refuge, and a space for collective work. Their vision is radical and radically ambitious: they are abolitionists committed to dismantling prisons and redirecting their funding to education and the repair of inequality. Their ultimate goal is to create in the present a future that overthrows the logic of neoliberalism.

These students are demonstrating how we might remake the world. They are ruthless in their criticism and fearless in the face of the powers that be. They model what it means to think through crisis, to fight for the eradication of oppression in all its forms, whether it directly affects us or not. They are *in* the university but not *of* the university. They work to understand and advance the movements in the streets, seeking to eliminate racism and state violence, preserve black life, defend the rights of the marginalized (from undocumented immigrants to transfolk), and challenge the current order that has brought us so much misery. And they do this work not without criticism and self-criticism, not by pandering to popular trends or powerful people, a cult of celebrity or Twitter, and not by telling lies, claiming easy answers, or avoiding the ideas that challenge us all.

"Barack Obama—The End of an Illusion" from

From #BlackLivesMatter to Black Liberation (2016)

Keeanga-Yamahtta Taylor

Keeanga-Yamahtta Taylor is a scholar, author, and activist who writes and speaks on Black politics, social movements, and racial inequality in the United States. In her 2016 book From #BlackLivesMatter to Black Liberation, *Taylor shows how the Black political establishment—in the case of the excerpt below, through the lens of the Obama presidency—has historically been unwilling to "address the effects of structural inequality" and ultimately short-circuited the potential transformative power of the movement that brought candidate Obama to office.*

Even while Black people endured the effects of the 2008 economic crisis, particularly the continuation of home foreclosures and double-digit unemployment, there was optimism that [Barack] Obama's election could change the course. Even before Obama was elected, there had been great optimism about what a Black presidency could mean for American racial politics. National Public Radio hosted a roundtable titled "A New, 'Post-Racial' Political Era in America" several months before the 2008 election.

President Obama turned out to be very different from candidate Obama, who had stage-managed his campaign to resemble something closer to a social movement. In the heated race for the Democratic nomination, Obama distinguished himself from establishment candidate Hillary Clinton by campaigning clearly against the war in Iraq and vowing to shut down the Guantánamo military internment camp. He spoke of economic inequality and connected with young people who were underwhelmed at the prospect of voting for yet another old, white windbag in John McCain. Black people's enthusiasm for the Obama campaign cannot be reduced to racial solidarity or recrimination. Obama electrified his audiences. . . .

In March 2008 Obama finally gave a comprehensive speech on race, in which he pulled off the feat of addressing the concerns of African Americans while calming the fears of white voters. That he broached the topic at all meant his speech was wildly misinterpreted by liberals and the mainstream media alike as further left of center than it actually was. . . .

No one running for president of the United States had ever spoken so directly about the history of racism in government and society at large. Yet Obama's speech also counseled that a more perfect United States required African Americans "taking full responsibility for our own lives . . . by demanding more from our fathers, and spending more time with our children, and reading to them, and teaching them that while they may face challenges and discrimination in their own lives, they must never succumb to despair or cynicism; they must always believe that they can write their own destiny." Obama couched his comments in the language of American progress and the vitality of the American dream, but the speech was remarkable nonetheless in the theater of American politics, where cowardice and empty rhetoric are the typical fare. In that sense Obama broke the mold, but he also established the terms upon which he would engage race matters—with dubious evenhandedness, even in response to events that required decisive action on behalf of the racially aggrieved. . . .

Before Ferguson, Obama's Philadelphia speech was as close as he had ever come to speaking truthfully about racism in the United States, even though he presented himself as an interested observer, a thoughtful interlocutor between African Americans and the nation as a whole, rather than a US senator with the political influence to effect the changes of which he spoke. Obama would continue in his role as "informed observer" even as president. We are led to believe that a man who can direct drone strikes in the mountains of Pakistan and Afghanistan, who can mobilize resources to any corner of the world in the name of American foreign policy, is powerless to champion legislation and the enforcement of existing laws and rights in the interest of racial justice. . . .

. . . Early in his administration, however, with the full effects of the recession still pulsing in Black communities, conflict between the Black president and his base could be detected. Black America was in the midst of an "economic free fall" and with it the disappearance of Black wealth. As Black unemployment was climbing into the high double digits, civil rights leaders asked Obama if he would craft policies to address Black joblessness. He responded, "I have a special responsibility to look out for the interests of every American. That's my job as president of the United States. And I wake up every morning trying to promote the kinds of policies that are going to make the biggest difference for the most number of people so that they can live out their American dream." It was a disappointing response, even if that disappointment did not manifest in his approval ratings. In 2011, with Black unemployment above 13 percent, 86 percent of Blacks approved of the overall job the president was doing, but 56 percent expressed disappointment in the "area of providing proper oversight for Wall Street and the big banks." Only half of Blacks said Obama's policies had improved the nation's economic condition. For African Americans, Obama's presidency had been largely defined by his reluctance to engage with and directly address the ways that racial discrimination was blunting the impact of his administration's recovery efforts.

Obama has not shown nearly the same reticence when publicly chastising African Americans for a range of behaviors that read like a handbook on anti-Black stereotypes, from parenting skills and dietary choices to sexual mores and television-watching habits. These public admonishments work to close off the political space within which African Americans can express legitimate grievances about an economic recovery that has offered material relief to bankers and auto executives but only moral uplift to Black people. Their cries for relief have been met with quips that Obama is "not the president of Black America." . . .

There is something disingenuous in focusing on poor and working-class Blacks without any discussion about the ways that the criminal justice system has "disappeared" Black parents from the lives of their children. When Obama talks about absentee Black fathers, he never mentions the disparity in arrests and sentencing that is responsible for the disproportionate number of missing Black men. Few media discussions about Obama's candidacy mentioned curbing the nation's criminal justice system's voracious appetite for Black bodies, but the scars of "law and order" were all over the Black body politic: a million

African Americans incarcerated; 10 percent of the Black formerly incarcerated prevented from voting; and one in four of Black men (in the age group twenty to twenty-nine) are under control of the criminal justice system. "Postracial" America was disappearing under an avalanche of disparities throughout the criminal justice system.

Over the course of his first term, Obama paid no special attention to the mounting issues involving law enforcement and imprisonment, even as Michelle Alexander's *The New Jim Crow* described the horrors that mass incarceration and corruption throughout the legal system had inflicted on Black families. None of this began with Obama, but it would be naive to think that African Americans were not considering the destructive impact of policing and incarceration when they turned out in droves to elect him. His unwillingness to address the effects of structural inequality eroded younger African Americans' confidence in the transformative capacity of his presidency....

The murder of Trayvon Martin in Sanford, Florida, in the winter of 2012 was a turning point. Like the murder of Emmett Till nearly fifty-seven years earlier, Martin's death pierced the delusion that the United States was postracial. Till was the young boy who, on his summer vacation in Mississippi in 1955, was lynched by white men for an imagined racial transgression. Till's murder showed the world the racist brutality pulsing in the heart of the "world's greatest democracy."...

No one knew who would be the next Trayvon, but the increasing use of smartphone recording devices and social media seemed to quicken the pace at which incidents of police brutality became public. These tools being in the hands of ordinary citizens meant that families of victims were no longer dependent on the mainstream media's interest: they could take their case straight to the public. Meanwhile, the formation of organizations dedicated to fighting racism through mass mobilizations, street demonstrations, and other direct actions was evidence of a newly developing Black left that could vie for leadership against more established—and more tactically and politically conservative—forces. The Black political establishment, led by President Barack Obama, had shown over and over again that it was not capable of the most basic task: keeping Black children alive. The young people would have to do it themselves.

"Introduction" from

Abolition. Feminism. Now. (2022)

Angela Y. Davis, Gina Dent, Erica R. Meiners, and Beth E. Richie

In the spirit of abolitionist feminist practice, abolitionist thinkers Angela Y. Davis, Gina Dent, Erica R. Meiners, and Beth E. Richie collectively wrote the boundary-pushing title Abolition. Feminism. Now. *Drawing from areas of thought such as carceral studies, abolition studies, and Black feminism,* Abolition. Feminism. Now. *makes the case that "a truly intersectional, internationalist, abolitionist feminism" ought to serve as a tool for building a world beyond the violence of carcerality and the repressiveness of raced and gendered state power.*

Abolition feminism *is* our political moment. After the racist execution carried out in Minneapolis, Minnesota, by uniformed representatives of state power and recorded on cell phones by bystanders, the name of George Floyd echoed around the world. How also to echo the murders and ongoing assaults on Asian and Asian American women, or the violent arrests of Black trans people, the detention of Latinx and other immigrant children at "the border," or the disappearance of women in Ciudad Juárez, Mexico? Even though for the first time in our memory, officials almost immediately declared the police killing of George Floyd to be a "murder" and the mass murder of Asian women in Atlanta in 2021 to be a "hate crime," the collective awakening was occasioned by the fact that tens of millions and perhaps more witnessed the last nine minutes of George

Floyd's life and the clear targeting of Asian women. Even for those who may be unfamiliar with the history of racist violence in the United States, these scenes aroused the historical specter of lynching and femicide. But this time, we were all implicated. And to fail to respond was tantamount to implicit assent. As we prepare this manuscript for publication, like the vast numbers of protesters and those sympathizing with activists in the streets throughout the world, we are still reeling from the sense that historical time has fast-forwarded, even as the present illuminates how much we are still held captive by unresolved questions from the past.

This collective moment has been ushered in through a long trajectory of campaigns, mobilizations, and actions, often precipitated by violence and death. Although we know the names of vast numbers of Black men who have lost their lives to police violence, the women, gender nonconforming people, trans people, and sex workers who are killed are most often relegated to the background. During the period preceding the murder of George Floyd, Breonna Taylor, a young Black woman who worked as an emergency medical technician, was executed by police in Louisville, Kentucky, as they entered her residence on a no-knock warrant apparently issued because she was a prior acquaintance of a person sought by the police. Breonna Taylor was in bed with her boyfriend when the police broke into her house and shot her eight times. If the name of George Floyd summons an unending list of Black men who have been targets of racist state violence—in the most recent era, Mike Brown, Eric Garner, Freddie Gray, Walter Scott, Philando Castile, and many others—the names of women are often erased, with the exceptions of Breonna Taylor, Sandra Bland, Rekia Boyd, and a few others.

George Floyd's murder became a major catalyst for abolitionist demands in large part because of prior radical organizing. In 2012, just days after her twenty-first birthday, CeCe McDonald was arrested for defending herself against racist and transphobic street violence. As she faced a charge of murdering her attacker and a lengthy prison sentence, a small but significant queer, trans, and mostly young multiracial network raised the visibility of her case through social media and organized street actions and workshops. This support was especially important during the nineteen months CeCe, a Black trans woman, was being held in a men's prison. CeCe and the campaign that emerged around her also worked to name all the ways the criminal legal system serves as an apparatus of repression against people on the peripheries of society, particularly trans people of color. This organizing surrounding CeCe, almost a decade before the summer 2020 uprising, elucidated the ideological connections between state violence, street violence, and interpersonal violence, a conjunction at the heart of all of the work of abolition feminism....

Of the many inspirations for the work of abolitionists today, one of the most important is a text that circulated widely among lay scholars and thinkers affiliated with the Black movement before it became part of the academic canon in the 1980s. W. E. B. Du Bois's *Black Reconstruction in America: An Essay Toward a History of the Part Which Black Folk Played in the Attempt to Reconstruct Democracy in America, 1860–1880* was published in 1935, a moment of social and political reckoning much like the one we are experiencing today. Written when there was an opening to new possibilities in the wake of capitalist crisis, Du Bois's volume on the history of post-slavery Radical Reconstruction and its demise not only reframed the period by centralizing Black agency in the making of a new democracy but also invited his contemporary readers to observe the crushing counterrevolutionary force of the property-holding elites. He argued that enslaved persons and free Black subjects were instrumental in the abolition of slavery, that slavery was indeed the cause of the Civil War, and that Reconstruction was more than a negation of slavery (and therefore was perceived as a threat by white property holders). His analysis offers a challenge both *to* historians of the period and *for* the present in which he wrote. These arguments also forecast the following contemporary abolitionist approaches: 1) taking leadership from those who are most directly impacted, so that the work incorporates the perspectives of the system's direct targets and not simply their more comfortably situated defenders; 2) calling for dismantling institutions that are overtly causing social and civil death; 3) broadening the liberatory agenda to include apparatuses of oppression beyond those that are specifically understood to be carceral; and 4) linking contemporary abolition praxis—or theory plus action and reflection—to questions of racial capitalism.

"Introduction: Black Health Matters" from *Black Disability Politics* (2022)

Sami Schalk

Sami Schalk is an interdisciplinary scholar and public intellectual whose work focuses broadly on disability, race, and gender in contemporary US literature and culture. Excerpted from her book Black Disability Politics, *the following passage outlines the aims of Black disability studies, problematizes disability as a historically white racialized discourse, and argues that disability studies must be radically reenvisioned if it is to "fully account for the ways disability politics manifest in Black communities and activism."*

... Merging scholarship, theories, and methods from disability studies and Black studies, as well as from postcolonial studies and feminist studies, especially Black feminist theory, Black disability studies explores both the lives of Black disabled people and the relationship between race and (dis)ability as systems of privilege and oppression. Black disability studies scholarship traces how disability has appeared among Black people, how disability has been treated and understood within Black communities, and how Blackness and disability have been—and continue to be—discursively linked in various cultures. As this field continues to develop and expand beyond the boundaries of the United States, scholars such as Christopher Bell, Nirmala Erevelles, Therí A. Pickens, Moya Bailey, myself, and others have increasingly demonstrated the ways that disability, as an identity, an experience, and a political category, has been conceptualized and approached differently by Black activists and intellectuals than by white activists and intellectuals, thereby requiring changes in scholarly and activist methods and frameworks.

For instance, there is a common narrative in disability studies that Black people have distanced themselves from concepts of disability and disability identity because of the way discourses of disability have been used to justify racist oppression. This narrative is often connected in the field with Douglas Baynton's frequently cited article "Disability and the Justification of Inequality in American History." The article's central thesis is that disability appears all over American history if we simply look closely enough. However, Baynton is often cited more specifically for his argument that marginalized groups, such as Black people, women, and immigrants, had discourses of disability foisted on them as justification for their exclusion from full rights and citizenship. In response, Baynton argues, these groups distanced themselves from disability as a means of accessing certain rights and freedoms. By distancing themselves from disability, he further contends, these other marginalized groups left unquestioned the notion that people with disabilities do not deserve full rights and citizenship, thereby passively accepting that disability is a justifiable rationale for discrimination and exclusion.

Baynton's article, which I myself frequently cite and teach, is incredibly important and useful; however, its narrative has become in some ways canon in the field of disability studies, used to explain why Black art, culture, and politics use disability merely as a metaphor for the impact of racism and often fail to incorporate disability politics, culture, or pride as typically understood in white disability studies and the disability rights movement. This narrative of Black distancing from disability is not wholly untrue, as much scholarship has demonstrated. However, disability studies scholars often use this narrative about Black people's relationship to disability without considering two key factors: first, the whiteness and racism of the disability rights movement and disability studies as a field, which often excludes or alienates Black disabled people; and, second, the possibility that disability politics may actually exist in Black activism and cultural work but manifest and operate in ways that do not look the same as disability politics in the mainstream movement. Recent work in Black disability studies demonstrates the multiple complex and nuanced ways that Black people, historically and contemporarily, have engaged with disability beyond simple distancing or denial. Collectively, my colleagues in Black disability studies have made clear that the narrative of Black disavowal of disability is merely a convenient, partial narrative that has remained underquestioned and underexplored within disability studies as a whole....

Further, disability justice is an inherently intersectional approach. Patty Berne writes that disability justice understands white supremacy and ableism as "inextricably entwined, both forged in the crucible of colonial conquest and capitalist domination." Disability justice values the leadership of those most impacted (i.e., multiply marginalized disabled people), anticapitalism, cross-movement organizing, sustainability, cross-disability solidarity, interdependence, collective access, and collective liberation. Practitioners of disability justice recognize that their work "already connects and overlaps with many movements and communities' work," especially work by feminist and queer people of color within reproductive justice, transformative justice, and healing justice movements. Disability justice work brings important knowledge, theory, and practices to contemporary antiracist activism. A disability justice framework also reveals how the disability rights movement has overlooked or dismissed Black activism around disability....

... Relatedly, disability justice activists "are building an analysis that includes political and historical understandings of disability, bodies, ableism, pace, illness, care, cure, aging, the medical industrial complex and access." Disability justice activists often include terms like *sick* and *chronically ill* to acknowledge and include people who may not identify as disabled, especially those who have been made sick or ill by white supremacist and heteropatriarchal violence and neglect. Similarly, crip theorist Alison Kafer describes disability as an expansive "political, and therefore contested and contestable category" and argues for recognizing the collective affinities among disabled, impaired, sick, ill, and Mad people, who are connected not by essential or inherent qualities but by the related oppressions we experience for our nonnormative bodyminds. These two similar approaches to disability as a political and social concern matter because disability studies and the disability rights movement have each often focused on apparent physical and sensory disabilities rather than on cognitive and mental disabilities or chronic illnesses. As Kafer notes, this "oversight is all the more troubling given the fact that diabetes occurs disproportionately" among racial minorities and that "asthma is a common side-effect of living in heavily polluted neighborhoods, which, un-surprisingly, are more likely to be populated by poor people." In other words, existing disability studies and disability rights frameworks for understanding and defining disability have been developed with little attention to the types of disability most common in poor and racialized communities. These white disability studies frameworks therefore are unable to fully account for the ways disability politics manifest in Black communities and activism.

PART THREE

HOW
WE
FIGHT
BACK

When Black Studies Is Contraband, We Must Be Outlaws

BREA BAKER

> The greatest threats to our freedom are hopelessness, help-
> lessness, and the criminalization of rebellion.
> —**Derecka Purnell**, *Becoming Abolitionists: Police, Protests,*
> *and the Pursuit of Freedom*

O n the morning of February 26, 2012, I was a senior in high school with plans to study physics at my dream college the following fall. Less than twenty-four hours later, Trayvon Martin had been murdered and, suddenly, everything changed.

For the first few months, I joined the country in a naive prayer hoping that the criminal legal system would "do its job." In July 2013, I held my breath as the jury read its verdict of "not guilty," acquitting Martin's killer of both charges. I was angry. I protested on my Yale campus, in New York City, and alongside my sister and other Howard students in Washington, DC. I switched my major from physics to undecided because sitting in a laboratory while Black people were being surveilled, hunted, and killed no longer felt like the way I wanted to spend my time. Taking action made me feel less idle, but I remained in a constant state of rage.

In some ways, I wore my fury as a badge of honor. To have death and devastation all around me and remain unscathed would have been far more concerning. But the anger was all-consuming and threatened to leave me so pessimistic as to throw up my hands in surrender. Yet, I come from survivors, innovators, and resisters. Giving up would have gone against everything I know.

I turned to elders and ancestors for guidance: *The Autobiography of Mal-*

colm X as told to Alex Haley. *The New Jim Crow* by Michelle Alexander. James Baldwin's *The Fire Next Time*. *Beloved* and *The Bluest Eye* by Toni Morrison. *Native Son* by Richard Wright. *Assata: An Autobiography* by Assata Shakur. *This Bridge Called My Back,* the anthology. Maya Angelou's *I Know Why the Caged Bird Sings*. White peers asked me for recommendations, and I led them to those same books, as well as works like *How to Be an Antiracist* by Ibram X. Kendi and *So You Want to Talk About Race?* by Ijeoma Oluo.

I wasn't the only one. As the #BlackLivesMatter movement became the vanguard of grassroots Black liberation work, millions around the nation rushed to read and learn and take action with this newfound awareness. And it worked. As Rashawn Ray wrote for the Brookings Institute, "Black Lives Matter helped illuminate the inordinate amount of money spent on policing," spurred policy shifts locally and federally, and shifted the norms we have around public safety.[1]

First, a Black president; then a Black-led social justice movement. The powers-that-be cracked down and their whitelashing gave way to the imprisonment of Black activists and a Trump presidency. We fought back again—harder. Black people organized rallies and spoke words that reflected the urgency of the moment. Books like *Caste* by Isabel Wilkerson, *All Boys Aren't Blue* by George M. Johnson, *The 1619 Project* by Nikole Hannah-Jones, *The Black Friend* by Fred T. Joseph, *We Do This 'Til We Free Us* by Mariame Kaba, and *Hood Feminism* by Mikki Kendall.

People weren't just reading. Asian and Pacific Islander people were coming together to wrestle with the legacy of anti-Blackness and were reviving solidarity ties between our communities. Latine people were addressing intra-community colorism and racism. White people were setting up mutual aid networks, reading abolitionist texts together, and putting their bodies on the line. Interfaith coalitions were decrying the moral failures of institutionalized racism and an American dream built on our backs. Corporations were being forced by employees and consumers alike to put their money where their mouths were. Black families were organizing for their land back and other measures of reparations—and winning!

Writers helped to ignite new imaginations of what is politically possible and organizers ran with it. What Toni Cade Bambara said about artists making the revolution irresistible had proven true as people of all backgrounds rushed to join the chorus of voices affirming the value of Black lives. It was a beautiful time of organizing against white supremacy and capitalism.

Again, the powers-that-be looked on in disgust, searching for a way to uproot the organizing well underway. In the land of free speech, the best way to smother radical public education is through institutions where people access and process a diversity of thought: schools, libraries, jails, and prisons. First, they came for the high-profile Black authors and most people treated it like a conservative fad. Then, Florida governor Ron DeSantis came for AP African American History and Black studies and Republicans nationwide followed his blueprint.

One of the most vital ways for us to resist is to get and read these banned books. Young people—or people working with young people—can look to the Brooklyn Public Library, which offers free eCards to anyone around the country and IPS/EyeSeeMe's Banned Book Program, which sends physical books directly to parents and children.

Of course, we can't have an abolitionist movement without being in community with those currently in the belly of the beast. In an effort to support those inside who are dealing with the immense violence of the prison system, Haymarket's Books Not Bars Program connects incarcerated people with radical books and opportunities for political education. Similarly, Noname Book Club's Prison Program has sent more than seventeen thousand books to over four hundred detention facilities across the country.

Young people can and should engage in a range of actions in their schools, on their campuses, with their loved ones, and in peer-led spaces detached from adult-led institutions. They can organize teach-ins, book clubs, film watch parties, and events geared at lobbying local school boards and state agencies. Until Freedom launched a digital educational series soon after the first wave of bans were announced in 2023. The pilot program, "You Gon' Learn Today," included sessions on early African history, maroonage/marronage, reparations, the US Constitution, radical love, and much more.

The Dream Defenders were among the first to lead the way toward an on-the-ground, youth-powered resistance effort. "School walkouts and teach-ins have been successfully used to change the course of our country's future, from the East L.A. walkouts by Mexican American students, to the Occidental College walkouts organized by student athletes, to the Moton High School walkouts and more," they wrote.[2] Through their #CantBanUs campaign, Dream Defenders have coordinated student walkouts and rallies in Florida and across the country. In parks, faith spaces, and other community sites, Dream Defenders and their allies hosted events to facilitate meaningful conversation around banned books and the ideologies they most want to keep from us.

On May 3, 2023, the Dream Defenders joined other leading racial justice organizations in a national day of action. That same day, the African American Policy Forum (AAPF), led by Kimberlé Crenshaw, took action through the Freedom to Learn initiative. Crenshaw coined the term *intersectionality* and was an early exponent of critical race theory, which have since become villainized, willfully misunderstood, and weaponized. Her scholarship not only makes people feel seen but has also created a framework for more justice in the legal system, so Crenshaw knows the power of words intimately. "Now is the time to work to build a broad coalition of people to strengthen our democracy and our values of equity, inclusion and social justice," AAPF wrote in the Freedom to Learn sign-up sheet.[3] AAPF and partners led read-alongs, banned-book giveaways, picketing, community town halls, and more.

This is just the beginning. This has to be just the beginning. Bestselling (and regularly banned) author Nic Stone has a tattoo of Black revolutionaries' mugshot numbers on her forearm:

7053 for Rosa Parks
7089 for Dr. Martin Luther King Jr.
22843 for Malcolm X.
51178 for Huey P. Newton
101464 for Doris Payne

Stone got the tattoo after being banned the first time "as a reminder of the trouble some of [her] heroes got into for being unapologetically themselves and openly championing what was important to them."[4] The concept of civil disobedience developed precisely because unjust laws must be broken by justice-seeking people. If our history has always been contraband, then we must be outlaws for liberation. We must read, learn, and organize our way to a more just future.

Brea Baker is an activist and writer who believes deeply in the need for Black storytelling and culture as a tool for change. She contributes essays on race, gender, and sexuality to publications like *ELLE, Harper's BAZAAR, Refinery*

29 *Unbothered, People, Coveteur, THEM, Mission Magazine,* and more. Brea's book *Rooted: The American Legacy of Land Theft and the Modern Movement for Black Land Ownership* is forthcoming from One World in 2024. You can learn more about her at BreaBaker.com.

History Is a Beautiful, Ugly Story, and We Must Teach It

MARLON WILLIAMS-CLARK

W
hen I first entered teaching, it became quickly apparent that Black students wanted to know more about their own history. As a graduate of Florida A&M University, an HBCU (historically Black college or university), I was eager to share with students the knowledge I'd obtained while in college about the Black experience. Fellow teachers would tell me that my students were bringing the information they learned in my class into their other classes; it was helping them to be better writers, inquisitors, and scholars. This filled me with joy because I knew that when students have a better understanding of where they come from, it makes them stronger people. Marcus Garvey stated that "a people without knowledge of their past history, origin, and culture is like a tree without roots." As students had questions, I sometimes gave impromptu Black history lessons. Before we knew it, the bell would ring for the next class period. This was often my experience when I taught at majority Black schools.

When I switched to a majority white school with a majority white faculty, there was a noticeable difference. Mouths said one thing, actions said another. I was, for the first time, questioned about my qualifications as a teacher during some of my first encounters with parents. Maybe this was because I was new, maybe it was because I was not what some parents were expecting: a young, confident, Black man. Fortunately, I was assigned a mentor teacher who was a Black woman, and, more importantly, a phenomenal educator. She helped me navigate some of the racism I encountered. I wanted to leave within a year of teaching there, but God had other plans for me. I didn't yet realize it, but my classes would become a safe haven for many Black and Brown students to express their thoughts and ask questions that they didn't feel they could broach with other teachers.

I have heard many anecdotes from Black and white students that made concrete the importance of teaching and engaging with Black history. Black students have told me that a white teacher once stated to them that when someone breaks into their home, they could call Black Lives Matter, while he would call the police. I've been told that another teacher compared Black women to cars when demonstrating slave auctions. Students recall teachers having them pick cotton when talking about slavery. Black students have been called monkeys and apes by their classmates, sometimes within earshot of the teacher. White baseball players have thrown the *n* word around in front of the one Black baseball player without regard, leaving that Black player feeling somewhat helpless to speak up. Incidents like this were foreign to me because I'd gone to a middle school and high school with majority Black students and faculty. I understood that I had to deconstruct a mythologized history of America that talks about freedom, liberty, and exceptionalism while simultaneously erasing the perspectives and experiences of Black people. And now there is an attempt by government officials across the nation to go even further to turn back the hands of time, reducing Black history to nothing more than a speck. It has been especially challenging to be an educator in Florida, where the AP African American Studies course was banned, and where other legislation has scared teachers and school librarians into eliminating most of their Black history material.

To talk about the importance of teaching Black history (and the pushback), we must be honest about ourselves and talk about values; values shape what one thinks is important to preserve. The history of Black people throughout the African diaspora has been riddled with stereotypes, myths, and miseducation. Dr. Carter G. Woodson spoke about those values in his 1933 book *The Mis-Education of the Negro*. Because of what Black people had been told about themselves, even professors at Negro schools did not want to include classes about Black history. Marcus Garvey, who rallied for Black people to move back to Africa, had a mindset that Black Americans were going back to the motherland to civilize it. Because of this negative mindset about Black people throughout the diaspora, anything that pushes for Black perspectives is labeled as radical or extremist. White supremacy can produce internalized racism where people belonging to an oppressed group take on the mindset and teachings of the oppressor about themselves. *The mere fact that African American history courses are elective speaks to the devaluation of a history that is othered and made controversial.* Black history is not radical, Black history *is* American history. As Angela Davis has noted, "If, indeed, we wish to be radical in our quest for change—then we must get to the root of our oppression. After all, *radical* simply means 'grasping things at the root.'" But *radical* has been used to describe perspectives that challenge the power structures of society and the history that comes with it. Some misinterpret that criticism as hate for America, but it is the opposite. Having different perspectives and viewpoints of history allows us to learn how to be better people; and critiquing one's country based on lived experiences is not hate but a love so strong that one dares criticize this country to make it better, a more perfect union as stated in the preamble of the Constitution.

At every step of the colonization of the "new world," Black people have been there. Like Langston Hughes expresses in his poem "The Negro Speaks of Rivers," Black people have been around and contributed to the world since the beginning of human society. As LaGarrett J. King expresses, we must move "away from policies that promote historical uniformity (all histories are the same) and historical integration (add Black people into history without serious consideration of their voices and perspectives) to more historical contentiousness (a history that is comfortable with competing perspectives about the ethos of America)."[1]

The last part is extremely important: a history that is comfortable with competing perspectives of the American ethos. The first two, historical uniformity and historical integration, have usually meant what the majority is comfortable with and historical references to Black achievements without context. US history is often taught in a propagandistic way, and, as we see with the pushback against the AP African American Studies pilot course, a decidedly white-centered way. I have witnessed in my own classes that when given the opportunity to discuss and debate differing views and perspectives, students become better for it. They are given the opportunity to learn from each other's differing realities and perspectives. Furthermore, they can become better debaters, learning how to support their arguments. However, healthy debate is not the only benefit to teaching Black history; it gives us a deeper and fuller accounting of how and why America upholds rights for some and denies them to others. It continues the conversation about making America "a more perfect union." For America to survive, it must be a work in progress.

We must teach the beautiful, ugly story that is American history, which includes experiences, identities, perspectives, joys, sorrows, and contributions of Black people. Teacher prep programs at the college level must do a better job of immersing our future teachers in Black history if we are going to have more accurate telling of our history—and I say *our* because Black history isn't only for Black people. Additionally, Black people must take up their own history to make sure that we in the United States never forget that Black people have been here, aren't going anywhere, and have pushed this country to embody the values and rights it proclaims for all Americans. Like Dr. Marvin Dunn, who started a bus tour of Black history sites and stories in Florida, we must become curators of our history and use our Black institutions to teach kids and adults alike about Black history. We must start our own weekend academies and after-school programs that place emphasis on the African American experience and the African diaspora. We cannot rely on a school system that otherizes Black history and upholds white supremacy through exclusion.

Black Americans have always understood the importance of having their own institutions, such as Prince Hall Masonic Lodges, the African Methodist Episcopal church, HBCUs, and the NAACP. In the early era of the civil rights movement, Septima Clark developed workshops called Citizenship Schools, noting that "literacy means liberation." Citizenship schools would inspire the Student Non-violent Coordinating Committee (SNCC) to develop Freedom Schools in Mississippi in the summer of 1964. Freedom Schools were a six-week program with an emphasis on reading, writing, math, history, and civics with the goal of preparing disenfranchised Black Americans to become politically active in a myriad of ways. The Black Panther Party (BPP) organized liberation schools with the understanding that the civil rights legislative achievements of the 1960s did not mean an immediate shift toward equality. The BPP's after-school programs eventually became the Oakland Community School. And BPP programs, developed to benefit Black communities, were so successful that today every public school in the nation retains part of its legacy in the form of the free and reduced lunch program.

Citizenship Schools, Freedom Schools, and BPP Liberation Schools are all part of the legacy of Black-led institution-building in service of Black freedom.

We can learn from—and perhaps even replicate—many of these examples in our own day. As Black communities work to build their own institutions to teach true histories, they also must knock down the doors of the school and school board meetings to push school districts to embrace and teach history accurately and to provide a safe learning space for our kids, or face lawsuits for denying our students' heritage and *our* parental rights. Black teachers make up a small percentage (around 7 percent) of the teacher workforce, and it can be exhausting. However, if Black teachers, ally teachers, Black parents, and community members start holding our school systems accountable as well as taking up measures to build up our children and broken adults (as Frederick Douglass told us in 1855), then we'll begin to heal, thrive, and rise. White people will have a better understanding that history affects the present, and it might not be comfortable; but it will be informative—and essential. It will break down the notion that slavery and the denigration of Black people just happened long ago. James Baldwin said, "History is not the past. It is the present. We carry our history with us. We are our history." And once we understand that, maybe I'll stop hearing my students ask: "Why didn't we learn that in US history?

Marlon Williams-Clark—known affectionately by his students as Mr. WC—has been an educator for over a decade. He currently teaches African American history at a high school in Florida and was one of sixty teachers across the country to pilot the College Board's AP African American Studies course. It is his goal to raise his students into well-rounded, diverse, and prepared citizens of society. One day, when his students are adults, they'll say, "Mr. WC prepared me for this."

In the Spirit of the Midnight School

RODERICK A. FERGUSON

In the introduction to Gloria T. Hull, Patricia Bell Scott, and Barbara Smith's authoritative anthology *All the Women Are White, All the Blacks Are Men, But Some of Us Are Brave*, the editors tell the story of an enslaved woman named Lily Ann Granderson. Granderson founded a clandestine school for blacks in Natchez, Mississippi. A "midnight school," the people called it. She started her classes at twelve at night and ended them at 2:00 a.m. The archive says, "Her number of scholars was twelve at a time, and when she had taught these to read and write, she dismissed them, and again took her apostolic number and brought them up to the extent of her ability, until she had graduated hundreds. A number of them wrote their own passes and started for Canada."[1]

In a moment in which conservative forces rally to suppress knowledge and the diverse groups of people who receive, rearticulate, and disseminate it, Mrs. Granderson's midnight schools provide us with the crucial principles needed for this historic challenge. In these dead-of-night lessons, we find an early instance of the classroom outside the classroom and the inspired activation of everyday people as the agents of collective liberation. This is the radical legacy that we must harness and reactivate.

The history of social movements provides spectacular examples of similar interventions. In this country, we need only look to the Mississippi Freedom Schools that challenged the racist domination of the all-white Mississippi Democratic Party and contested white supremacy through a curriculum taught by young Black and white student volunteers from colleges and universities around the country—volunteers who would run their Freedom Schools in basements, in churches, on porches, and under trees. We need only study the

Black radical reading groups in the Bay Area that the historian Donna Murch discusses in her book *Living for the City: Migration, Education and the Rise of the Black Panther Party in Oakland, California.* Talking about one group, the African American Association (AAA), she writes, "Through a wide and varied reading list that brought together cultural anthropology, critical black sociology, and classic works in African American history, the AAA politicized a whole generation of black students who passed through Bay Area colleges and universities in the late fifties and early sixties."[2] In addition, we simply have to take inspiration from Street Transvestite Action Revolutionaries (S.T.A.R.), that organization founded by the Stonewall veterans Sylvia Rivera and Marsha P. Johnson, who used their S.T.A.R. house on 213 East Second Street in New York to practice mutual aid and to raise such questions as, "Why do we suffer?" and "Why do we got to take the brunt of this shit?"[3] These are just a few of the many examples.

Behind these interventions was a steadfast commitment to the power of nonelites. Indeed, the great organizer and leader Ella Baker said in a 1969 speech at the Institute of the Black World, "We have to begin to think in terms of where do we really want to go and how do we get there.... [One] of the guiding principles has to be that we cannot lead a struggle that involves masses of people without identifying with the people and without getting the people to understand what their potentials are, what their strengths are."[4] In his 1963 "Letter from Birmingham City Jail," Dr. Martin Luther King sounded a note like Baker's. He said, "Nonviolent direct action seeks to create such a crisis and establish such creative tension that a community that has consistently refused to negotiate is forced to confront the issue. It seeks so to dramatize the issue that it can no longer be ignored."[5] For Baker and King, ordinary people would largely be the channels for new kinds of social, political, and intellectual potentials and creativities—potentials and creativities that society needed for a life-and-death confrontation.

Our present conjuncture requires us to extend these legacies of direct action and community activation. Doing so involves identifying and establishing the institutions and collectivities through which we can foster creative tensions, forms of knowledge, and genres of strength—in schools, neighborhoods, churches, mosques, cell blocks. It means learning from and multiplying organizations made up of progressive teachers and parents like the Anti-racist Teaching and Learning Collective. It entails coordinating curricular efforts across K–16. It presumes supporting the 153 black bookstores listed on the African American Literature Book Club's website. It concerns holding up public and independent libraries like the Eastside Freedom Library in St. Paul, Minnesota.

If the right is terrified of a politically astute population, winning means seriously proliferating the opportunities for critical political education. Whether through reading groups, community organizations, bookstores, or libraries, we can turn these into relays for progressive know-how and analysis. And if there are places with none of these institutions, we can create them.

In her book *No Shortcuts: Organizing for Power in the New Gilded Age*, the organizer and author Jane McAlevey draws on histories of direct action to identify "the agency for success with a continually expanding base of ordinary people, a mass of people never previously involved, who don't consider themselves activists at all—that's the point of organizing."[6] She also writes, "When people understand the strategy because they helped to make it, they will be invested for the long haul, sustained and propelled to achieve more meaningful wins."[7] By contrast, those organizations that privilege elites are most often characterized by short-term victories. As she states, "Many small advances can be and are won without engaging ordinary people, where the key actors are instead paid lawyers, lobbyists, and public relations professionals, helped by some good smoke and mirrors. That is an advocacy model, and small advances are all it can produce."[8] Building a movement with ordinary people—at its heart—entails creating new social relations, and there can be no shortcuts when it comes to that.

As dismaying as our present catastrophe is, this could be the moment of a political shift that returns us to the fundamentals of direct action and the broad activation of critical pedagogies. Such a return is necessary because we have become overtrained in seeking celebrity and wealth as the presumed means for effecting change. As a result, we have forgotten that the most crucial strategy involves looking for the sister, brother, or sibling in the neighborhood who— on those hot-ass summer days—controls the fire hydrant.

Roderick A. Ferguson is professor of Women's, Gender, and Sexuality Studies at Yale University. He is the author of *One-Dimensional Queer* (Polity, 2019); *We Demand: The University and Student Protests* (University of California, 2017); *The Reorder of Things: The University and Its Pedagogies of Minority Difference* (University of Minnesota, 2012); and *Aberrations in Black: Toward a Queer of Color Critique* (University of Minnesota, 2004). He is the coeditor with Grace Hong of the anthology *Strange Affinities: The Gender and Sexual Politics of Comparative Racialization* (Duke University, 2011). He is also coeditor with Erica Edwards and Jeffrey Ogbar of *Keywords of African American Studies* (NYU, 2018). He is currently working on two monographs—*The Arts of Black Studies* and *The Bookshop of Black Queer Diaspora*.

Acknowledgments

This book originated in response to the attacks on the teaching of Advanced Placement African American Studies in Florida and the broader efforts to ban books, whitewash history, and roll back civil and human rights.

We want to thank Carmen Rojas, Zeeba Khalili, and the remarkable team at Marguerite Casey Foundation for their collaboration from the earliest stages of this work, which made our accelerated schedule of production possible, and is allowing us to publish *Our History Has Always Been Contraband: In Defense of Black Studies* as a free ebook and to give away copies in print to students, educators, and organizers confronting these attacks.

Everyone at Kaepernick Publishing and Haymarket Books worked on a highly compressed schedule to publish this book. We especially want to thank Christopher Petrella, Dao X. Tran, and Anthony Arnove for their editorial work and invaluable commitment to this effort, and Rachel Cohen for her extensive work reviewing archival photos with us and helping us envision a compelling cover and interior design.

Thanks to our contributors to this book. We are extremely honored to include original essays by Brea Baker, Roderick A. Ferguson, and Marlon Williams-Clark. And we are deeply moved by the authors who granted us permission to include their previously published work, as well as the many individuals who have supported this project with their quick attention to permissions requests. We especially want to thank Ellen Adler, George Andreou, Margot Atwell, Frances M. Beal, Stuart Bernstein, Dean Birkenkamp, Mary Brower, Linda Burnham, Federico Campagna, Deborah Chasman, Sumi Cho, Jennifer Civiletto, Monique Corea, Angela Y. Davis, Gina Dent, Rebecca Eskildsen, the Estate of Octavia E. Butler, George Gibson, Merrilee Heifetz, Suzanne Herz, Lauren Rosemary Hook, Winston Oliver Huff, Mary Beth Jarrad, Sut Jhally, Jonathan Karp, Trysha Le, Geri Thomas Lemert, Peter London, Maria Martinez, John McLeod, Erica R. Meiners, Jeffery Moen, Cherríe Moraga, Sandra

Mullings, John Oakes, Kerin Ogg, Gayatri Patnaik, Norah Perkins, Barbara Ransby, Beth E. Richie, Yessenia Santos, Laure Schlink, John Sherer, Mia Silva, Barbara Smith, Karma B. Smith, Amy Sun, Sharon Swados, Alia Tyner, Michael Tyner, Hannah Vose, Stephanie Vyce, and Abby West.

Kaepernick Publishing wishes to thank Milo Dodson; Haymarket extends special thanks to Jim Plank and Katy O'Donnell; and the Marguerite Casey Foundation sends gratitude to Mackenzie Kwok and the team at Camino for helping to amplify this project.

And a special thanks to the teachers, students, and others organizing to defend Black Studies at this critical moment in our history.

Permissions

Notes

On Racial Justice, Black History, Critical Race Theory, and Other Felonious Ideas

1. Manny Diaz Jr. (@SenMannyDiazJr), "Despite the Lies from the Biden White House, Florida Rejected an AP course," Twitter, January 20, 2023, 5:35 p.m., infographic, https://twitter.com/SenMannyDiazJr/status/1616565048767385601.
2. Stop W.O.K.E. ACT, www.myfloridahouse.gov/Sections/Documents/loaddoc. aspx?FileName=h0007z1.JDC.DOCX&DocumentType=Analysis&BillNumber=0007&Session=2022.
3. Anemona Hartcollis and Eliza Fawcett, "The College Board Strips Down Its A.P. Curriculum for African American Studies," *New York Times*, February 1, 2023, www.nytimes.com/2023/02/01/us/college-board-advanced-placement-african-american-studies.html; Pema Levy, "The College Board Just Watered Down Its New AP African American History Course," *Mother Jones*, February 1, 2023, www.motherjones.com/politics/2023/02/ap-african-american-history-ron-desantis/; Fabiola Cineas, "The Controversy Over AP African American Studies, Explained," *Vox*, February 9, 2023, www.vox.com/policy-and-politics/23583240/ap-african-american-studies-college-board-florida-ron-desantis; Eesha Pendharkar, "AP African American Studies: How Other States Are Responding after Florida's Ban," *Education Week*, February 23, 2023, www.edweek.org/teaching-learning/ap-african-american-studies-how-other-states-are-responding-after-floridas-ban/2023/02; quotation from Prem Thakker, "Florida Repeatedly Contacted the College Board About the A.P. African American Studies Course," *New Republic*, February 9, 2023, https://newrepublic.com/post/170530/florida-repeatedly-contacted-college-board-watered-ap-african-american-studies.
4. Becky Sullivan, "With a Nod to '1984,' a Federal Judge Blocks Florida's Anti-'woke' Law in Colleges," NPR, November 18, 2022, www.npr.org/2022/11/18/1137836712/college-university-florida-woke-desantis-1984; Ben Brasch, "Judge Nixes Higher Education Portions of Florida's Stop WOKE Act," *Washington Post*, November 22, 2022, www.washingtonpost.com/nation/2022/11/17/judge-nixes-higher-education-portions-floridas-stop-woke-act/.
5. Dana Goldstein and Stephanie Saul, "The College Board Will Change Its A.P. African American Studies Course," *New York Times*, April 24, 2023, www.nytimes.com/2023/04/24/us/ap-african-american-studies-college-board.html.
6. See Peter P. Hinks, ed. *David Walker's Appeal to the Coloured Citizens of the World*

(University Park: Pennsylvania State University Press, 2000).

7.   Jarvis R. Givens, *Fugitive Pedagogy: Carter G. Woodson and the Art of Black Teaching* (Cambridge, MA: Harvard University Press, 2021), 4; See also Drusilla Dunjee Houston, "Why Negroes Reject Negro History," *Atlanta Daily World*, September 2, 1934.

8.   Jon N. Hale, *The Freedom Schools: Student Activists in the Mississippi Civil Rights Movement* (New York: Columbia University Press, 2017); Karen Joyce Cook, "Freedom Libraries in the 1964 Mississippi Freedom Summer Project: A History," (PhD dissertation, University of Alabama, 2008); see also, Derecka Purnell, "America Has a History of Banning Black Studies. We Can Learn from That Past," *Guardian*, February 14, 2023, www.theguardian.com/commentisfree/2023/feb/14/african-american-studies-history-repression-resistance-republicans.

9.   See Martha Biondi, *The Black Revolution on Campus* (Los Angeles and Berkeley: University of California Press, 2012); Abdul Alkalimat, *The History of Black Studies* (London: Pluto Press, 2021); Fabio Rojas, *From Black Power to Black Studies: How a Radical Social Movement Became an Academic Discipline* (Baltimore: Johns Hopkins University Press, 2007); Stefan M. Bradley, *Harlem vs. Columbia University: Black Student Power in the Late 1960s* (Urbana: University of Illinois Press, 2009); Nathaniel Norment Jr., *African American Studies: The Discipline and Its Dimensions* (New York: Peter Lang, 2019); William M. Banks, *Black Intellectuals: Race and Responsibility in American Life* (New York: W. W. Norton, 1996); Russell Rickford, *We Are an African People: Independent Education, Black Power, and the Radical Imagination* (New York: Oxford University Press, 2015); Noliwe M. Rooks, *White Money/Black Power: The Surprising History of African American Studies and the Crisis of Race in Higher Education* (Boston: Beacon Press, 2006); Ibram X. Kendi, *The Black Campus Movement: Black Students and the Racial Reconstitution of Higher Education, 1965–1972* (New York: Palgrave Macmillan, 2012); Nicholas O. Mitchell, "Disciplinary Matters: Black Studies and the Politics of Institutionalization" (PhD dissertation, University of California, Santa Cruz, 2011); Gary Y. Okihiro, *Third World Studies: Theorizing Liberation* (Durham, NC: Duke University Press, 2016); Roderick A. Ferguson, *We Demand: The University and Student Protests* (Oakland: University of California Press, 2017); Greg Carr, "What Black Studies Is Not: Moving from Crisis to Liberation in Africana Intellectual Work," *Socialism and Democracy* 25, no. 1 (March 2011): 178–91; Robin D. G. Kelley, "Over the Rainbow: Third World Studies Against the Neoliberal Turn," in *Reflections on Knowledge, Learning and Social Movements: History's Schools*, eds. Aziz Choudry and Salim Vally (London and New York: Routledge, 2018), 205–22.

10. Chuck Morse, "Capitalism, Marxism, and the Black Radical Tradition: An Interview with Cedric Robinson," *Perspectives on Anarchist Theory* (Spring 1999), 8.

11. What has come to be known as "the history wars" in the US has a very long history. For an excellent account written by combatants in this war (the founders of the National Center for History in the Schools at UCLA, which came under fire from conservatives in the 1990s when it sought to change the national history standards), see Gary B. Nash, Charlotte Crabtree, and Ross E. Dunn, *History on Trial: Culture Wars and the Teaching of the Past* (New York: Vintage, 2000); and also see Jonathan Zimmerman, *Whose America? Culture Wars in the Public Schools* (Cambridge, MA: Harvard University Press, 2005). Nine years ago, when a new group of scholars and teachers revised the US advanced placement class by including more about social

conflict, race and gender, the ideology of Manifest Destiny, slavery as a catalyst for the Civil War, and questioning "American exceptionalism," conservatives attacked the new curriculum for being "divisive" and emphasizing the "negative aspects of our nation's history while omitting or minimizing positive aspects." Republicans called for a congressional investigation, and some state legislatures voted to ban AP US History altogether, ultimately forcing the College Board to make further revisions in order to satisfy conservatives. Adam B. Lerner, "History Class Becomes a Debate on America," *Politico*, February 21, 2015, www.politico.com/story/2015/02/ap-us-history-controversy-becomes-a-debate-on-america-115381; Libby Nelson, "How Conservatives Forced Changes to AP US History to Make It More "pro-American," *Vox*, August 3, 2015, www.vox.com/2015/8/3/9089245/ap-us-history-controversy; Michael Hiltzik, "Education Watch: Oklahoma Legislature Votes to Dumb Down Its Kids," *Los Angeles Times*, February 18, 2015, www.latimes.com/business/hiltzik/la-fi-mh-oklahoma-kids-20150217-column.html.

12. See, for example, Micki McElya, *Clinging to Mammy: The Faithful Slave in the Twentieth-Century* (Cambridge, MA: Harvard University Press, 2007); Kristin Hass, *Blunt Instruments: Recognizing Racist Cultural Infrastructure in Memorials, Museums, and Patriotic Practices* (Boston: Beacon Press, 2023); Robin D. G. Kelley, "We're Getting These Murals All Wrong," *Nation*, September 10, 2019, https://www.thenation.com/article/archive/arnautoff-mural-life-washington/.

13. Citations of CRT associated with the late Derrick Bell, Kimberlé Crenshaw, Cheryl Harris, Richard Delgado, Patricia Williams, Gloria Ladson-Billings, Tara Yosso, Mari Matsuda, among others.

14. Taifha Alexander, LaToya Baldwin Clark, Kyle Reinhard, and Noah Zatz, *CRT Forward: Tracking the Attack on Critical Race Theory* (Los Angeles: UCLA Critical Race Studies, 2023), 10; see also, Benjamin Wallace-Wells, "How a Conservative Activist Invented the Conflict over Critical Race Theory," *New Yorker*, June 18, 2021, www.newyorker.com/news/annals-of-inquiry/how-a-conservative-activist-invented-the-conflict-over-critical-race-theory.

15. Alexander et al., *CRT Forward: Tracking the Attack on Critical Race Theory*, 9.

16. Alexander et al., *CRT Forward: Tracking the Attack on Critical Race Theory*, 4, 6–7.

17. Sarah Schwartz, "Who's Really Driving Critical Race Theory Legislation?" *Education Week*, July 19, 2021, www.edweek.org/policy-politics/whos-really-driving-critical-race-theory-legislation-an-investigation/2021/07; Alexander et al., *CRT Forward: Tracking the Attack on Critical Race Theory*, 13. Henry Giroux is the leading scholar and critic of the right-wing war on schools and public education. He has published too much to cite here, but see especially Henry A. Giroux, *Insurrections: Education in an Age of Counterrevolutionary Politics* (London: Bloomsbury Academic, 2023); "DeSantis's Educational Policies Come Right Out of the Fascist Playbook," *Counterpunch*, March 3, 2023, www.counterpunch.org/2023/03/03/desantiss-educational-policies/; "Attacks on Critical Race Theory Seek to Insert Fascist Politics into Education," *Truthout*, September 4, 2021, https://truthout.org/audio/attacks-on-critical-race-theory-seek-to-insert-fascist-politics-into-education/; "Right-Wing Authoritarianism and the Crisis of Education," *Counterpunch*, December 10, 2021, www.counterpunch.org/2021/12/10/right-wing-authoritarianism-and-the-crisis-of-education/.

18. These same "divisive concepts" appear in the vast majority of bills, with only slight alterations. Those quoted come mainly from New Hampshire House Bill 544 and

Florida's Stop WOKE Act (cited above). "Bill Text: NH HB544," https://legiscan.com/NH/text/HB544/id/2238380; Jaclyn Peiser, "N.H. Governor Slams Conservative Group's $500 Reward for Reporting Critical Race Teachings: 'Wholly Inappropriate,'" *Washington Post*, November 19, 2021; Wallace Hettle, "Keep History Teachers Free to Teach, in Iowa and the Nation," *History News Network*, June 20, 2021, https://historynewsnetwork.org/article/180574.

19. Alexander et al., *CRT Forward: Tracking the Attack on Critical Race Theory*, 6–7.

20. Florida House of Representatives, CS/HB 999, "A Bill to Be Entitled an Act Relating to Postsecondary Educational Institutions," March 15, 2023, 4–7.

21. Florida House of Representatives, CS/HB, 2, 13–15, 18; Divya Kumar, "Florida Bill Would End Diversity Programs, Ban Majors, Shift Power at Universities," *Tampa Bay Times*, February 23, 2023, www.tampabay.com/news/education/2023/02/23/florida-bill-would-end-diversity-programs-ban-majors-shift-power-universities/; The Adam Smith Center for Economic Freedom, https://freedom.fiu.edu/.

22. The President's Advisory 1776 Commission, *The 1776 Report*, January 2021, 18, https://trumpwhitehouse.archives.gov/wp-content/uploads/2021/01/The-Presidents-Advisory-1776-Commission-Final-Report.pdf.

23. The original series of essays appeared in the *New York Times Magazine*, August 14, 2019, www.nytimes.com/interactive/2019/08/14/magazine/1619-america-slavery.html, but since then it has expanded into a book-length collection of essays by an even more varied group of scholars. See Nikole Hannah-Jones, Caitlin Roper, Ilena Silverman, and Jake Silverstein, eds., *The 1619 Project: A New Origin Story* (New York: Random House, 2021).

24. C. A. Bridges, "What Is 'The 1619 Project' and Why Has Governor DeSantis Banned It from Florida Schools?" *Tallahassee Democrat*, January 27, 2023, /www.tallahassee.com/story/news/education/2023/01/27/1619-project-hulu-why-are-republican-states-banning-it-in-schools/69847374007/.

25. The President's Advisory 1776 Commission, *The 1776 Report* (January 2021), 8–12, https://trumpwhitehouse.archives.gov/wp-content/uploads/2021/01/The-Presidents-Advisory-1776-Commission-Final-Report.pdf.

26. *The 1776 Report*, 15.

27. Martin Luther King Jr., *Why We Can't Wait* (New York: Harper and Row, 1963), 147.

28. Martin Luther King Jr., "Remaining Awake through a Great Revolution," in *A Testament of Hope: The Essential Writings and Speeches of Martin Luther King, Jr.*, ed. James M. Washington (New York: HarperCollins Publishers, 1986), 268–78.

29. Martin Luther King Jr., "Honoring Dr. Du Bois," *Jacobin*, January 21, 2019, https://jacobin.com/2019/01/web-du-bois-martin-luther-king-speech.

30. Ishena Robinson, "Anti-CRT Mania and Book Bans Are the Latest Tactics to Halt Racial Justice," Legal Defense Fund, https://www.naacpldf.org/critical-race-theory-banned-books/?gclid=CjwKCAjwitShBhA6EiwAq3RqA7nCmVkUxz9XwQSv6rkC07qMh8QPFsRdmwFukwDS5aeSsSVlbw-gmxoCGlMQAvD_BwE.

Black Studies Is Political, Radical, Indispensable, and Insurgent

1. "Remarks by President Trump at the White House Conference on American History," September 17, 2020, https://trumpwhitehouse.archives.gov/briefings-state-

ments/remarks-president-trump-white-house-conference-american-history.

2. Manny Diaz, Jr. (@SenMannyDiazJr), "Despite the Lies from the Biden White House, Florida Rejected an AP course," Twitter, January 20, 2023, 5:35 p.m., https://twitter.com/SenMannyDiazJr/status/1616565048767385601.

3. Patricia Mazzei and Anemona Hartocollis, "Florida Rejects A.P. African American Studies Class," *New York Times*, January 19, 2023, www.nytimes.com/2023/01/19/us/desantis-florida-ap-african-american-studies.html.

4. Eesha Penharkar, "A.P. African American Studies: How Other States Are Responding after Florida's Ban," *Education Week*, February 23, 2023, www.edweek.org/teaching-learning/ap-african-american-studies-how-other-states-are-responding-after-floridas-ban/2023/02.

5. Robert Allen, "Politics of the Attack on Black Studies," *Black Scholar* 6, no. 1 (1974): 2–7.

6. Allen, "Politics of the Attack on Black Studies."

7. Allen, "Politics of the Attack on Black Studies."

8. Juan Perez Jr. and Nicole Gaudiano, "Trump Blasts 1916 Project as DeVos Praises Black History Curriculum," *Politico*, September 17, 2020, www.politico.com/news/2020/09/17/devos-black-history-1776-unites-417186.

9. "Read Trump's Prepared Remarks at the 2020 RNC," *Politico*, August 27, 2020, www.politico.com/news/2020/08/27/trump-rnc-speech-transcript-404061.

10. "Read Trump's Prepared Remarks."

11. Scott Walker (@ScottWalker), "Younger voters may be behind the stinging loss for conservatives in WI," Twitter, April 6, 2023, 1:03 p.m., https://twitter.com/ScottWalker/status/1644023052001222686.

12. "Executive Order on Establishing the President's Advisory 1776 Commission," November 2, 2020, https://trumpwhitehouse.archives.gov/presidential-actions/executive-order-establishing-presidents-advisory-1776-commission.

13. "Executive Order on Establishing the President's Advisory 1776 Commission."

14. "Executive Order on Establishing the President's Advisory 1776 Commission."

15. Allen, "Politics of the Attack on Black Studies."

When Black Studies Is Contraband, We Must Be Outlaws

1. Rashawn Ray, "Black Lives Matter at 10 Years: 8 Ways the Movement Has Been Highly Effective," Brookings Institution, October 12, 2022, www.brookings.edu/blog/how-we-rise/2022/10/12/black-lives-matter-at-10-years-what-impact-has-it-had-on-policing.

2. Dream Defenders, *Can't Ban Us: February 23 National Day of Action Toolkit*, https://www.canva.com/design/DAFaEjkwWtg/view?utm_content=DAFaEjkwWtg&utm_campaign=designshare&utm_medium=embeds&utm_source=link.

3. "Freedom to Learn National Day of Action Sign-up Sheet," Google doc, https://docs.google.com/forms/d/e/1FAIpQLSduJkdCq8i6PGEOfrLR2eQw8ZDffx-DW_aJtVZpKcgQsgPAXVQ/viewform.

4. Nic Stone (@nicstone), Instagram post, photo, March 4, 2023, https://www.instagram.com/p/CpYSBs-gojw/?utm_source=ig_web_copy_link.

History Is a Beautiful, Ugly Story, and We Must Teach It

1. LaGarrett J. King, "Black History Is Not American: Toward a Framework of Black Historical Consciousness," *Social Education* 86, no. 6 (2020): 340.

In the Spirit of the Midnight School

1. Gloria T. Hull, Patricia Bell Scott, and Barbara Smith, *All the Women Are White, All the Blacks Are Men, But Some of Us Are Brave* (New York: Feminist Press, 1982), xix.
2. Donna Jean Murch, *Living for the City: Migration, Education and the Rise of the Black Panther Party in Oakland, California* (Chapel Hill: University of North Carolina, 2010), 96.
3. "'I'm Glad I Was in the Stonewall Riot': An Interview with Sylvia Rivera," *Street Transvestite Action Revolutionaries: Survival, Revolt, and Queer Antagonist Struggle*, edited by Ehn Nothing (Untorelli Press), 13.
4. Ella Baker, "The Black Woman in the Civil Rights Struggle—the Long View: A Speech Given at the Institute of the Black World in Atlanta, 1969." chrome-extension://efaidnbmnnnibpcajpcglclefindmkaj/https://www.crmvet.org/info/69_baker_speech-c.pdf.
5. Martin Luther King Jr., "Letter from Birmingham City Jail," in *The Essential Writings and Speeches of Martin Luther King, Jr.*, ed. James M. Washington (New York: HarperCollins, 1986), 291.
6. Jane McAlevey, *No Shortcuts: Organizing for Power in the New Gilded Age* (Oxford: Oxford University Press, 2016), 10.
7. McAlevey, *No Shortcuts*, 6.
8. McAlevey, *No Shortcuts*, 6.

Recommended Readings in Black Studies

Abdul Alkalimat, *The History of Black Studies*

Robert L. Allen, *Black Awakening in Capitalist America: An Analytic History*

David Austin, *Moving Against the System: The 1968 Congress of Black Writers and the Making of Global Consciousness*

James Baldwin, *The Fire Next Time*

———, *No Name in the Street*

Toni Cade Bambara, ed., *The Black Woman: An Anthology*

Mia Bay, Farah Jasmine Griffin, Martha S. Jones, and Barbara Dianne Savage, eds, *Toward an Intellectual History of Black Women*

Ruha Benjamin, *Race after Technology: Abolitionist Tools for the New Jim Code*

Steve Biko, *I Write What I Like*

Martha Biondi, *The Black Revolution on Campus*

Keisha N. Blain, *Set the World on Fire: Black Nationalist Women and the Global Struggle for Freedom*

Keisha N. Blain and Ibram X. Kendi, eds., *Four Hundred Souls: A Community History of African America, 1619–2019*

Joshua Bloom and Waldo E. Martin Jr., *Black Against Empire: The History and Politics of the Black Panther Party*

James Boggs and Stephen M. Ward, *Pages from a Black Radical's Notebook: A James Boggs Reader*

Gwendolyn Brooks, *Maud Martha*

Scot Brown, ed., *Discourse on Africana Studies: James Turner and Paradigms of Knowledge*

Octavia Butler, *Kindred*

Aimé Césaire, *Discourse on Colonialism*

Patricia Hill Collins, *Black Feminist Thought: Knowledge, Consciousness and the Politics of Empowerment*

Anna Julia Cooper, *A Voice from the South*

James H. Cone, *A Black Theology of Liberation*

Kimberlé Crenshaw, Neil Gotanda, Gary Peller, and Kendall Thomas, eds., *Critical Race Theory: The Key Writings That Formed the Movement*

Angela Y. Davis, *Abolition Democracy: Beyond Empire, Prisons and Torture*

———, *Angela Davis: An Autobiography*

———, *The Meaning of Freedom and Other Difficult Dialogues*

Angela Y. Davis, Gina Dent, Erica R. Meiners, and Beth E. Richie, *Abolition. Feminism. Now.*

Thulani Davis, *The Emancipation Circuit: Black Activism Forging a Culture of Freedom*

Michael C. Dawson, *Black Visions: The Roots of Contemporary African-American Political Ideologies*

St. Clair Drake, *Black Folk Here and There: An Essay in History and Anthropology*

W. E. B Du Bois, *The Souls of Black Folks*

Erica R. Edwards, Roderick A. Ferguson, and Jeffrey O. G. Ogbar, eds., *Keywords for African American Studies*

Ralph Ellison, *Invisible Man*

Adam Ewing, *The Age of Garvey: How a Jamaican Activist Created a Mass Movement and Changed Global Black Politics*

Frantz Fanon, *Black Skin, White Masks*

———, *The Wretched of the Earth*

Ashley D. Farmer, *Remaking Black Power: How Black Women Transformed an Era*

Johanna Fernández, *The Young Lords: A Radical History*

Vincent P. Franklin, *Black Self-Determination: A Cultural History of African-American*

Henry Louis Gates Jr., editor, *The Classic Slave Narratives*

Dan Georgakas and Marvin Surkin, *Detroit: I Do Mind Dying—
A Study in Urban Revolution*

Paula Giddings, *When and Where I Enter:
The Impact of Black Women on Race and Sex in America*

Ruth Wilson Gilmore, *Abolition Geography: Essays Towards Liberation*

Paul Gilroy, *The Black Atlantic: Modernity and Double Consciousness*

Édouard Glissant, *Poetics of Relation*

Michael A. Gomez, *Reversing Sail: A History of the African Diaspora*

Lewis R. Gordon, *Fear of Black Consciousness*

———, *Introduction to Africana Philosophy*

Farah Jasmine Griffin, *In Search of a Beautiful Freedom:
New and Selected Essays*

———, *Who Set You Flowin'?: The African-American Migration Narrative*

Alexis Pauline Gumbs, *Spill: Scenes of Black Feminist Fugitivity*

Beverly Guy-Sheftall, ed., *Words of Fire: An Anthology of African American
Feminist Thought*

Stuart Hall, *The Fateful Triangle: Race, Ethnicity, Nation*

Nikole Hannah-Jones, Caitlin Roper, Ilena Silverman, and Jake Silverstein,
eds., *The 1619 Project: A New Origin Story*

Vincent Harding, *There Is a River: The Black Struggle for Freedom in America*

Cheryl Harris, "Whiteness as Property"

Leonard Harris, ed. *Philosophy Born of Struggle: Anthology of Afro-American
Philosophy from 1917*

Saidiya Hartman, *Scenes of Subjection: Terror, Slavery,
and Self-making in Nineteenth-Century America*

Robert A. Hill and Barbara Bair, *Marcus Garvey: Life and Lessons:
A Centennial Companion to the Marcus Garvey
and Universal Negro Improvement Association Papers*

Chester Himes, *Lonely Crusade*

bell hooks, *Ain't I a Woman: Black Women and Feminism*

————, *Black Looks: Race and Representation*

————, *Yearning: Race, Gender, and Cultural Politics*

Gerald Horne, *The Counter-Revolution of 1776:*
   Slave Resistance and the Origins of the United States of America

Akasha (Gloria T.) Hull, Patricia Bell-Scott, and Barbara Smith, eds.
   All the Women Are White, All the Blacks Are Men,
   But Some of Us Are Brave: Black Women's Studies

Zora Neale Hurston, *Their Eyes Were Watching God*

Richard Iton, *In Search of the Black Fantastic:*
   Politics and Popular Culture in the Post-Civil Rights Era

George Jackson and Jonathan Jackson, *Soledad Brother:*
   The Prison Letters of George Jackson

Joy James, *Transcending the Talented Tenth:*
   Black Leaders and American Intellectuals

E. Patrick Johnson and Mae Henderson, eds., *Black Queer Studies:*
   A Critical Anthology

James Weldon Johnson, *The Essential Writings of James Weldon Johnson,*
   ed. Rudolph P. Byrd

Jacqueline Jones, *Labor of Love, Labor of Sorrow:*
   Black Women, Work and the Family, from Slavery to the Present

Martha S. Jones, *Vanguard: How Black Women Broke Barriers,*
   Won the Vote, and Insisted on Equality for All

Peniel E. Joseph, *Waiting 'Til the Midnight Hour:*
   A Narrative History of Black Power in America

Robin D. G. Kelley, *Freedom Dreams: The Black Radical Imagination*

Martin Luther King, Jr., *Where Do We Go from Here? Chaos or Community*

————, *The Radical King*, ed. Cornel West

Tiffany Lethabo King, *The Black Shoals:*
   Offshore Formations of Black and Native Studies

George Lamming, *In the Castle of My Skin*

George Lipsitz, *A Life in the Struggle: Ivory Perry and the Culture of Opposition*

Alain Locke, ed., *The New Negro*

Audre Lorde, *Sister Outsider: Essays and Speeches*

Manning Marable, *How Capitalism Underdeveloped Black America:
    Problems in Race, Political Economy, and Society*

Paule Marshall, *Brownstone, Brown Girls*

Kyle T. Mays, *An Afro-Indigenous History of the United States*

Katherine McKittrick, *Demonic Grounds:
    Black Women and the Cartographies of Struggle*

Katherine McKittrick and Clyde Woods, eds.,
    Black Geographies and the Politics of Place

Charles W. Mills, *The Racial Contract*

Toni Morrison, *Beloved*

———, *The Bluest Eye*

———, *Playing in the Dark: Whiteness and the Literary Imagination*

———, *Song of Solomon*

———, *Sula*

Fred Moten, *In the Break: The Aesthetics of the Black Radical Tradition*

Fred Moten and Stefano Harney, *The Undercommons:
    Fugitive Planning and Black Study*

Donna Murch, *Living for the City: Migration, Education,
    and the Rise of the Black Panther Party in Oakland, California*

Joshua Myers, *Of Black Study*

Nathaniel Norment, Jr., *African American Studies:
    The Discipline and Its Dimensions*

Paul Ortiz, *An African American and Latinx History of the United States*

Charles Payne, *I've Got the Light of Freedom*

Ann Petry, *The Street*

Barbara Ransby, *Ella Baker and the Black Freedom Movement*

———, *Making All Black Lives Matter:
    Reimagining Freedom in the Twenty-First Century*

Ishmael Reed, *Mumbo Jumbo*

Russell Rickford, *We Are an African People: Independent Education,*

Black Power, and the Radical Imagination

Dorothy Roberts, *Killing the Black Body: Race, Reproduction, and the Meaning of Liberty*

Cedric J. Robinson, *Black Movements in America*

———, *Forgeries of Memory and Meaning: Blacks and the Regimes of Race in American Theater and Film before World War II*

Walter Rodney, *How Europe Underdeveloped Africa*

David R. Roediger, *How Race Survived US History: From Settlement and Slavery to the Obama Phenomenon*

Fabio Rojas, *From Black Power to Black Studies: How a Radical Social Movement Became an Academic Discipline*

Assata Shakur, *Assata*

Christina Sharpe, *In the Wake: On Blackness and Being*

Manisha Sinha, *The Slave's Cause: A History of Abolition*

Barbara Smith, ed., *Homegirls: A Black Feminist Anthology*

Geneva Smitherman, *Talkin' and Testifyin': Language of Black America*

Hortense J. Spillers, *Black, White, and in Color: Essays on American Literature and Culture*

Brenda E. Stevenson, *What Is Slavery?*

Sterling Stuckey, *Slave Culture: Nationalist Theory and the Foundations of Black America*

Keeanga-Yamahtta Taylor, ed., *How We Get Free: Black Feminism and the Combahee River Collective*

Ula Yvette Taylor, *The Promise of Patriarchy: Women and the Nation of Islam*

Jeanne Theoharis, *A More Beautiful and More Terrible History: The Uses and Misuses of Civil Rights History*

———, *The Rebellious Life of Mrs. Rosa Parks*

Joe W. Trotter, *Workers on Arrival: Black Labor in the Making of America*

Cornel West, *Keeping Faith: Philosophy and Race in America*

Deborah Gray White, Mia Bay, and Waldo E. Martin, *Freedom on My Mind: A History of African Americans with Documents*

Frank B. Wilderson III, *Afropessimism*

———, *Red, White and Black: Cinema and the Structure of US Antagonism*

Clyde Woods, *Development Arrested: The Blues and Plantation Power in the Mississippi Delta*

Richard Wright, *Native Son*

———, *Black Boy*

Sylvia Wynter, "Unsettling the Coloniality of Being/Power/Truth/Freedom: Towards the Human, after Man, Its Over-representation—An Argument"

Malcolm X, with Alex Haley, *The Autobiography of Malcolm X*

About the Editors

Amari Kenoly for Kaepernick Publishing

Super Bowl QB **COLIN KAEPERNICK**, holder of the all-time NFL record for most rushing yards in a game by a quarterback, took a knee during the playing of "The Star-Spangled Banner" in 2016 to bring attention to systemic oppressions—specifically police terrorism—against Black and Brown people. For his stance, he has been denied employment by the league to this day.

Since 2016, he has founded and helped to fund three organizations—Know Your Rights Camp, Kaepernick Media, and Kaepernick Publishing—that together advance the liberation of Black and Brown people through storytelling, systems change, and political education.

In 2022, he became a *New York Times* bestselling author for his acclaimed children's picture book, *I Color Myself Different*, which explores transracial adoption through the lens of family and identity.

Courtesy of UCLA

ROBIN D. G. KELLEY is the Gary B. Nash Endowed Chair in US History at UCLA. His books include *Thelonious Monk: The Life and Times of an American Original*, *Hammer and Hoe: Alabama Communists During the Great Depression*, and *Freedom Dreams: The Black Radical Imagination*, recently released in a new twentieth anniversary edition.

His essays have appeared in several publications, including *The Nation*, *New York Times*, and *Boston Review*, for which he also serves as contributing editor.

Kelley's other books include *Africa Speaks, America Answers: Modern Jazz in Revolutionary Times, Yo' Mama's Disfunktional!: Fighting the Culture Wars in Urban America, Race Rebels: Culture, Politics, and the Black Working Class*, and *Into the Fire: African Americans Since 1970* (volume 10 of the Young Oxford History of African Americans series).

© Hannah Price

KEEANGA-YAMAHTTA TAYLOR writes and speaks on Black politics, social movements, and racial inequality in the United States. She is the author of *Race for Profit: How Banks and the Real Estate Industry Undermined Black Homeownership* and a 2021 MacArthur Foundation Fellow.

Her earlier book, *From #BlackLivesMatter to Black Liberation*, won the Lannan Cultural Freedom Award for an Especially Notable Book in 2016. She is also editor of *How We Get Free: Black Feminism and the Combahee River Collective*.

Taylor is a contributing writer at the *New Yorker* and a former contributing opinion writer for the *New York Times*.

For eight years, Taylor was professor of African American Studies at Princeton University. She is currently a professor in the Department of African American Studies at Northwestern University.

About Kaepernick Publishing

Founded by Colin Kaepernick in 2019, Kaepernick Publishing strives to elevate a new generation of writers with diverse views and voices through the creation of powerful works of all genres that can build a better and more just world.

MORE TITLES FROM KAEPERNICK PUBLISHING

Abolition for the People: The Movement for a Future without Policing and Prisons
Edited by Colin Kaepernick

The Bridges Yuri Built: How Yuri Kochiyama Marched across Movements
(coming April 2024)
By Kai Naima Williams
Illustrated by Anastasia Williams

Change the Game
By Colin Kaepernick and Eve L. Ewing
Illustrated by Orlando Caicedo

Dreamer
By Akim Aliu with
Greg Anderson Elysée

I Color Myself Different
By Colin Kaepernick
Illustrated by Eric Wilkerson

In the Blink of an Eye: An Autobiography
By Mahmoud Abdul-Rauf with Nick Chiles

About Haymarket Books

Haymarket Books is a radical, independent, nonprofit book publisher based in Chicago. Our mission is to publish books that contribute to struggles for social and economic justice. We strive to make our books a vibrant and organic part of social movements and the education and development of a critical, engaged, and internationalist Left.

We take inspiration and courage from our namesakes, the Haymarket Martyrs, who gave their lives fighting for a better world. Their 1886 struggle for the eight-hour day—which gave us May Day, the international workers' holiday—reminds workers around the world that ordinary people can organize and struggle for their own liberation. These struggles—against oppression, exploitation, environmental devastation, and war—continue today across the globe.

Since our founding in 2001, Haymarket has published more than nine hundred titles. Radically independent, we seek to drive a wedge into the risk-averse world of corporate book publishing. Our authors include Angela Y. Davis, Arundhati Roy, Keeanga-Yamahtta Taylor, Eve L. Ewing, Aja Monet, Mariame Kaba, Naomi Klein, Rebecca Solnit, Olúfẹ́mi O. Táíwò, Mohammed El-Kurd, José Olivarez, Noam Chomsky, Winona LaDuke, Robyn Maynard, Leanne Betasamosake Simpson, Howard Zinn, Mike Davis, Marc Lamont Hill, Dave Zirin, Astra Taylor, and Amy Goodman, among many other leading writers of our time. We are also the trade publishers of the acclaimed Historical Materialism Book Series.

Haymarket also manages a vibrant community organizing and event space in Chicago, Haymarket House, the popular Haymarket Books Live event series and podcast, and the annual Socialism Conference.

Also Available from Haymarket Books

Abolition. Feminism. Now.
by Angela Y. Davis, Gina Dent, Erica R. Meiners, and Beth E. Richie

Abolition for the People: The Movement for a Future Without Policing and Prisons
Edited by Colin Kaepernick

Angela Davis: An Autobiography
Angela Y. Davis

Assata Taught Me
State Violence, Racial Capitalism, and the Movement for Black Lives
Donna Murch

Community as Rebellion
A Syllabus for Surviving Academia as a Woman of Color
Lorgia García Peña

Elite Capture
How the Powerful Took Over Identity Politics (and Everything Else)
Olúfẹ́mi O. Táíwò

From #BlackLivesMatter to Black Liberation (expanded second edition)
Keeanga-Yamahtta Taylor, foreword by Angela Y. Davis

Not Too Late: Changing the Climate Story from Despair to Possibility
Edited by Rebecca Solnit and Thelma Young Lutunatabua

Black Women Writers at Work
Edited by Claudia Tate, foreword by Tillie Olsen

Rehearsals for Living
Robyn Maynard and Leanne Betasamosake Simpson
Foreword by Ruth Wilson Gilmore